T. S. Eliot, Wallace Stevens,
and the Discourses of Difference

T. S. Eliot, Wallace Stevens, and the Discourses of Difference

Michael Beehler

Louisiana State University Press
Baton Rouge and London

Designer: Christopher Wilcox
Typeface: Sabon
Typesetter: G & S Typesetters, Inc.
Printer: Thomson-Shore, Inc.
Binder: John Dekker & Sons, Inc.

Sections of Chapters One and Four have appeared, in different form, in *Genre*. An earlier version of a section of Chapter Two has been published in *Criticism,* and an early version of Chapter Six has appeared in *Wallace Stevens Journal*. Earlier versions of portions of Chapter Three have been published in *boundary 2* and *Bucknell Review*.

The author gratefully acknowledges Alfred A. Knopf, Inc., for granting permission to quote from *Letters of Wallace Stevens,* ed. Holly Stevens, copyright © 1966 by Holly Stevens; *The Collected Poems of Wallace Stevens,* copyright 1954 by Wallace Stevens; *Opus Posthumous,* ed. Samuel French Morse, copyright © 1957 by Elsie Stevens and Holly Stevens; *The Necessary Angel: Essays on Reality and the Imagination,* by Wallace Stevens, copyright 1951 by Wallace Stevens; and *Souvenirs and Prophecies: The Young Wallace Stevens,* by Holly Stevens, copyright © 1966, 1976 by Holly Stevens.

Publication of this book has been assisted by a grant from the Andrew W. Mellon Foundation.

Library of Congress Cataloging-in-Publication Data

Beehler, Michael.
   T. S. Eliot, Wallace Stevens, and the discourses of difference.

   Includes index.

   1. American poetry—20th century—History and criticism. 2. Eliot, T. S. (Thomas Stearns), 1888–1965—Criticism and interpretation. 3. Stevens, Wallace, 1879–1955—Criticism and interpretation. 4. Deconstruction. 5. Semiotics and literature. I. Title.
PS324.B4   1986   821'.912'09   86-11393
ISBN 0-8071-1269-0

For Helen, Bobb, and Sharon

Contents

Acknowledgments

I owe a special debt of gratitude to Joseph N. Riddel, my teacher for four years and my friend for many more. His critical insights first opened my eyes to the work of Stevens and Eliot and to the problems that could be articulated by a grafting of Continental literary criticism onto these giants of American modernism. Without his enthusiastic interest in my work, this book would never have been written. His work and his friendship continue to be an inspiration. I must also thank William V. Spanos for his careful and provocative reading of an early draft of the manuscript. His dialogue with my readings of Eliot have proved to be particularly productive.

Special thanks go to Beverly Jarrett at LSU Press for her support of the manuscript; to Elizabeth L. Carpelan for her meticulous editing and perceptive suggestions; to Carol Rhodes, for her flawless production of the typescript; and to the University of Texas, Austin, for a grant that financed the typing. My gratitude to Sharon for our many late-night critical debates could go without saying.

Abbreviations

Works by Eliot

CPP   *The Complete Poems and Plays: 1909–1950* (New York, 1971)

EE   *Elizabethan Essays* (London, 1934)

HF   Introduction to Samuel L. Clemens, *The Adventures of Huckleberry Finn* (London, 1959)

KE   *Knowledge and Experience in the Philosophy of F. H. Bradley* (New York, 1964)

MC   *Murder in the Cathedral* (New York, 1935)

OPP   *On Poetry and Poets* (New York, 1943)

SE   *Selected Essays* (London, 1950)

SW   *The Sacred Wood* (London, 1920)

UPUC   *The Use of Poetry and the Use of Criticism* (London, 1933)

Works by Stevens

CP   *The Collected Poems of Wallace Stevens* (New York, 1954)

LWS   *Letters of Wallace Stevens*, ed. Holly Stevens (New York, 1966)

NA   *The Necessary Angel: Essays on Reality and the Imagination* (New York, 1951)

OP   *Opus Posthumous*, ed. Samuel French Morse (New York, 1957)

T. S. Eliot, Wallace Stevens,
and the Discourses of Difference

The difference is part of the
thing itself, and perhaps it
even produces the thing. . . .
In the beginning was the noise.

—Michel Serres

Introduction
Insisting on Difference

For the past twenty years, the story of twentieth-century American
poetry has been the narrative of two distinct poetic expressions—
T. S. Eliot's and Wallace Stevens'—and has been guided by the figure of continuity. In *Poets of Reality*, for example, J. Hillis Miller
discloses the depth of the critical desire to include both poetries in a
tale of unity that will not minimize the differences between the two
writers but that nevertheless will gather up those differences into a
whole that allows them to be fruitfully explored. In his preface Miller asserts that Eliot and Stevens (as well as the other four poets of
reality—Conrad, Yeats, Dylan Thomas, and William Carlos Wil-
liams) begin "with an experience of nihilism or its concomitants,
and each in his own way enters the new reality." Thus Miller emphasizes the unity of twentieth-century poetry—a unity suggested
by and repeated in its differences.[1]

A similar emphasis guides Roy Harvey Pearce's earlier account,
The Continuity of American Poetry. Pearce traces in many American poets a "determining immanence" that makes meaningful their
differences, a unity he calls the "basic style" that underlies and
organizes the differing unique styles of the poems. His appeal to
this immanent identity is vital to his project, for in seeking to "com-

1. J. Hillis Miller, *Poets of Reality: Six Twentieth-Century Writers* (New York,
1974), 10, 11.

prehend as a continuing series the texts which do, or should, count most with us," his goal is to write a seamless story of American poetry and to account for difference by following a thread of essential, immanent identity that moves continuously through all its different temporal manifestations.[2]

The final chapters of Pearce's book trace this immanence in the now familiar differences between the mythic and Adamic phases of American poetry, in other words, in the differences between an Eliotic style and a Stevensian style that are, for Pearce, manifestations in two radically opposed ways of the basic style. Here the mythic Eliot and the Adamic Stevens are complements of each other, and the summation of their complementary styles yields for Pearce a vision of the coherent and continuous immanence in American poetry. Pearce calls Eliot and Stevens the two "great figures" of the "insistent opposition" immanent in American poetry's continuity: "the egocentric as against the theocentric, man without history as against history without man, the antinomian as against the orthodox, personality as against culture, the Adamic as against the mythic." This fundamental difference between Eliot and Stevens is contained, however, in what is for Pearce a higher and more original identity: "The basic style of both the adamic and the mythic poem has derived from the poet's concern to declare that language, in spite of all that we may do to it, is inherently meaningful—no matter what the ultimate source of meaning—because poems made out of it can manifest its capacity to mean." Thus, although Eliot and Stevens respond differently to one of Pearce's abiding questions, "Whence the authority?"—Eliot answers "God" whereas Stevens answers "Man"—the difference here is only in the names by which the authority of meaning is designated by the two poets.[3] When Pearce reads Eliot and Stevens, he sees in their difference a microcosmic repetition of his generalized scheme of American poetic history—a scheme in which the differences between unique styles are resolved by the identity of a basic style whose embodiments may be always different but whose meaning is always the same.

For Pearce, as for Miller and most other critics who read Eliot and Stevens side by side, the question of difference is answered before the critical project begins, and the answer relies upon a determining immanence that at some point in the discourse reconciles

2. Roy Harvey Pearce, *The Continuity of American Poetry* (Princeton, 1961), 13, 3.
3. *Ibid.*, 421, 433, 423, 431, 429.

the differences between the two poets. These differences are interpreted as representations or different versions of a fundamental identity or in-difference. It is in this question of difference and in the critical assumption that differences are reducible to an identity they embody that the following chapters seek to intervene. They will take difference in Eliot and Stevens as a repeatedly deployed problem that resists reductions to the simple identity of an essence or immanence.

Where Pearce writes of the "insistent opposition" that characterizes Eliot and Stevens, he can do so only within the homogenizing framework of the "basic style," and thus his emphasis upon opposition and difference can go only so far before it is resolved in a unifying solution. But if such insistent opposition is conceived of radically and allowed to interfere with all resolving conceptions of unity, then immanence must be thought of as irreducibly multiple. From this perspective, there can be no final solution to the question of difference, but only an endless redeployment of it. Thinking of difference in this way also leads to a reappraisal of the complementariness between Eliot and Stevens, for where the discourse of immanence sees different versions of the same basic style, a discourse of insistent difference emphasizes the manner in which this resolution is questioned by an irreducible proliferation of versions. From such a critical position, immanence cannot be thought of as a continuous essence moving through the differences that presumably represent it. Rather, it can only be thought of as the repeated deployment of difference; not, that is, as the re-presentation of the same, but as the recurrence of difference. Similarly, continuity must also be reconstituted, not as the progress of a basic style within the differences of unique styles, but as the discontinuous displacements and differentiations of a plurality of styles and versions irreducible to the constraints of a central identity. The following readings, then, seek to free difference in Eliot and Stevens from the homogenizing effects of figures of identity and to rethink the differences upon which their writings insist.

To approach Eliot and Stevens in this way is to ask other questions of their texts. For if our critical language insists upon displacing figures of essence and immanence by thinking of them only as problematic sites of difference, then we cannot, without deflecting our project, search in Eliot's incarnational and mythic rhetoric or in Stevens' fictive and Adamic language for the common elements upon which their differences close. Rather, we must accept diver-

gence and insist upon its disruptive reiteration to ask how it is repeatedly deployed and what its function is in each of these poetic
rhetorics, particularly in their varied appraisals of the status of
signs, representations, and poetic language itself. Any appeal to an
essential immanence must invariably be made from within a particular theory of representation, one which suggests that the differences between words close in the basic Word, that the detours of
metaphor arrive at a central literality, that the errors of fiction resolve themselves in the revelation of truth. But these chapters will
concentrate upon the question of signs and representation in Eliot
and Stevens in order to reiterate the insistent and centerless plurality
that marks in their figures of identity and their meditations on language the eternal return of a problem.

There is, of course, the unavoidable risk that, by tracing Eliot's
and Stevens' repeated deployments of difference, we render them indistinguishable. This risk, however, is a necessary component of our
argument, for if the repetition of insistent difference suggests on one
hand a homogenizing uniformity, it at the same time affirms difference as pure difference, as an incessantly heterogeneous and differentiating process without cognitive core or essential immanence.
The reiteration of difference, in other words, prohibits a reductive
thematization or conceptualization of difference; rather, it underscores the fundamental irreducibility of difference by allowing it
to resonate with identity as the doubled voice of a problem, one
ceaselessly redeployed rather than finally resolved. This book does
not, then, seek to distribute the distinctions between Eliot and
Stevens into individualized zones or categories, since such a distribution—for the purposes of comparison and contrast, for example—leads only to the obscuring of the differential process by
the categorizations the critical text, in its desire for mastery and
order, inevitably supplies. Thus we will attempt to avoid directly
asking the reductive question, "What is the difference between Eliot
and Stevens?" by displacing it with other questions that emphasize
the redeployments of difference as an insistent process—questions
of the status of difference, of how it is suppressed by an appeal to
immanence and identity, of where it is deployed as a structural necessity, and of how it is incessantly set circulating as irreducibly an-
archical and nomadic.

What right have we to intervene in the discourse of immanence and
representation with a discourse of difference? What effect does

such an intervention have on the poetries of Eliot and Stevens? And, most crucially, why Eliot and Stevens at all? Why reread these particular two poets, together, from this intervening and disruptive point of view?

To respond to these questions, we can begin by examining an array of texts that with varying degrees of explicitness encourage a rethinking of difference. These texts are interdisciplinary, drawn from philosophy, physics, and aesthetics as well as literary criticism. They suggest a historical and intertextual matrix that makes a discourse of difference seem not simply more probable, but even necessary.

Although we could enter this array at any point with any text, since what is at stake here is not historical continuity or influence, but rather the distribution of some notable points of difference, let us enter it through Stevens' 1943 essay, "The Figure of the Youth as Virile Poet." Written for *Les Entretiens de Pontigny* at Mount Holyoke College, the essay seeks, among other projects, to differentiate philosophy from poetry.

> As we come to the point at which it is necessary to be explicit in respect to poetic truth, note that if we say that the philosopher pursues the truth in one way and the poet in another, it is implied that both are pursuing the same thing, as we overlook the fact that they are pursuing two different parts of a whole. It is as if we said that the end of logic, mathematics, physics, reason and imagination is all one. In short, it is as if we said that there is no difference between philosophic truth and poetic truth. There is a difference between them and it is the difference between logical and empirical knowledge. (NA 53–54)

What Stevens rejects here is the implication of an epistemological immanence, a logical, universal truth that is the same thing for both philosophers and poets. Rejecting this immanence, Stevens forces us to think of the difference between philosophers and poets as irreducible, and thus of truth and knowledge as incessantly plural.

Within this plurality there emerge isolated localities of truth and knowledge or, more accurately, truths and knowledges—one for the philosopher and one for the poet. Each remains true in its own methodological sense and from its own local point of view, but there is for Stevens no neutral perspective from which to judge the ontological validity of these differing methodological constructions. Truth and knowledge, in other words, are never innocently neutral or objective, but are always produced by local points of view or local methodologies that are irreducibly different from each other. In fact, since the significance of these local truths cannot be specified by comparing them to a more essential and generalized truth, it is clear that the coherence of each relies only upon its difference from the other; that is, the philosopher's truth and the poet's truth have differential rather than absolute significance.

Because of this strictly differential significance of truths, when Stevens seeks to define the individualized essence of poetic truth, he presents that definition as a statement of strategic, rhetorical necessity and not of ontological validity. "It may be said that poetic truth is an agreement with reality, brought about by the imagination of a man disposed to be strongly influenced by his imagination, which he believes, for a time, to be true, expressed in terms of his emotions or, since it is less of a restriction to say so, in terms of his own personality. And so stated, the difference between philosophic truth and poetic truth appears to become final. As to the definition itself, it is an expedient for getting on." Indeed, when Stevens presents a definition of either poetic or philosophic truth—a definition which suggests that difference becomes final by being distributed into two articulated categories—he presents it only as "a statement of convenience" (NA, 54, 41). The importance of such definitions is strictly strategic: they construct the two individualized and incommensurable categories of thought in which the argument can operate while at the same time disclosing the methodological expediency of such individualization. The definitions of truth are not accorded anything but a formal significance or validity.

Stevens states that "in spite of the absence of a definition and in spite of the impressions and approximations we are never at a loss to recognize poetry. As a consequence it is easy for us to propose a center of poetry, a *vis* [screw] or *noeud* [knot] *vital*, to which, in the absence of a definition, all the variations of definition are peripheral." This supplementation distributes an otherwise undifferentiated field of definitions into a center and a periphery, and produces the definitions that then emerge as different and individualized. Like light, which Stevens later notes adds nothing to an undifferentiated field of darkness except itself, the supplemental center, without which there can only be an indistinguishable sameness in which there is nothing to see, produces the things that are different, or the various definitions of poetry (NA, 44–45, 61). It thus serves a strategic function, though not as a fixed essence, since it is always proposed in the absence of such a defining immanence; it is nevertheless irreducibly essential or vital as an expedient point of view, a convenient instrument whose rhetorical employment produces the differences on which vision (in the case of light) or argumentation (in the case of poetic definition) depend.

This differentiating procedure is what Stevens proposes as characteristic of the masculine nature of his virile figure. From its own convenient *noeud vital,* the essay has produced its methodologically different categories of truth, but at the end of the essay Stevens again liberates difference from the categories it produces. "We have been referring constantly to the simple figure of the youth, in his character of poet, as virile poet. The reason for this is that if, for the poet, the imagination is paramount, and if he dwells apart in his imagination, as the philosopher dwells in his reason, and the priest dwells in his belief, the masculine nature that we propose for one that must be the master of our lives will be lost as, for example, in the folds of the garments of the ghost or ghosts of Aristotle" (NA, 66–67). Aristotelian categorization, which can take place only upon an already differentiated field of individualized things, obscures the difference upon which it depends by apportioning that field into independent zones of coherence that, because they are taken as dwelling apart from each other, seem not to interfere with each other. It is from such reductive categorization and individualization that Stevens liberates difference.

When Stevens again differentiates between philosophers and poets in his 1951 essay "A Collect of Philosophy," he articulates their divergent use of concepts. "The habit of forming concepts [a "habit of the mind by which it probes for an integration"] unites them. The use to which they put their ideas separates them." The difference, Stevens concludes, lies in the fact that the "philosopher intends his integrations to be fateful; the poet intends his to be effective." The effective use of an integrating concept as a strategic "statement of convenience" rather than as an assertion of universal law or fate ties the poet to the quantum physicist, and Stevens closes his essay with a quotation from André George about Max Planck. Concerning the "thesis on causality," which should (and did, in Newtonian physics) function as an absolute, universal principle reducing the empirical differences between all physical events to a coherent, lawful, and fateful identity, George reads Planck as suggesting that such a physical law ("the rigorous causal bond between two successive events") "ought to be independent of man." But, as Planck points out, such a concept can be liberated from an "anthropomorphic hypothesis" only through the appeal to "an intelligence external to man" and "not constituting a part of nature" that would "act through the deterministic power." To interpret the thesis of causality as a universal principle, in other words, requires us to postulate it as a neutrally transcendent absolute on which the differences in man's interpretations and observations of physical events and the differences between the events themselves have no bearing, as, that is, a statement of fateful, rigorous law equivalent to what Stevens calls the universal maxims of Kant. But Stevens notes that it is precisely the "rigid determinism of classic science" that quantum theory has dispelled, and it is Planck himself who concludes that the law of casuality [sic] is neither true nor false. It is a working hypothesis" (OP, 196–97, 202).

Whereas classical physicists and philosophers see in their concepts the transcendent identity of universal law, quantum physicists and poets see only local statements of convenience or working hypotheses, experimental or rhetorical expedients allowing the experiment or the argument to get on. No natural immanence or basic law resolves the empirical differences between these methodological hypotheses; one cannot even arrive at immanence by adding up all the differences, since this leads only to the "gaucherie" of the *Monadology*, which, according to Stevens, reflects Gottfried Leibniz's project to achieve God "monad by monad . . . by way of the course of an immense unity." For Stevens, as for Planck, such integrating universal laws, the conceptual "big figures" of physics, philosophy, and poetry, are "statistical illusions" that play only instrumentally as an "aggregate of statistical compensations" for the differences they do not finally reconcile or control (OP, 185, 195).[4]

Thus Planck and Stevens share what Stevens suggests is an important "nuance of the imagination." Quantum physics does not seek a rigid determinism immanent in different empirical phenomena, but rather redeploys difference when it "calculates the measure of their respective probabilities." The modern physics Stevens found so instructive disperses the universality of conceptual laws into a dynamic field of irreducible difference, or in phrases Stevens uses to describe the implications of Alfred North Whitehead's rejection of

4. Wallace Stevens, "Three Manuscript Endings for 'A Collect of Philosophy,'" in Frank Doggett and Robert Buttel (eds.), *Wallace Stevens: A Celebration* (Princeton, 1980), 55, 56, 53, 56.

simple location, "a universal iridescence, a dithering of presences and, say, a complex of differences" (OP, 202, 192). This does not mean that physics and poetry can do without universalizing concepts, without expedient big figures, but that their rhetorical employment always suggests a problem. Such a conceptual identity is always a working hypothesis that *does work:* not the work of difference-reducing integration, but the work of differentiation, of making the differences vital to the discourses of both physics and poetry. Their employment, in other words, marks the eternal return of irreducible difference and of what Stevens characterizes as a fundamental indeterminacy. "Nature offers us on a grand scale a determinist aspect, thanks to the play of big figures, of statistical illusion. But on the atomic scale, at the level of elementary phenomena, an indeterminacy, fundamental and, it must be added, well-defined, reigns alone."[5]

Stevens' insistent thinking of difference places him in agreement with Cyril Joad's observation, quoted by the poet in "The Noble Rider and the Sound of Words," that "philosophy has long dismissed the notion of substance and modern physics has endorsed the dismissal," a statement that leads Joad to ask "How, then, does the world come to appear to us as a collection of solid, static objects extended in space? Because of the intellect, which presents us with a false view of it" (NA, 25). This dismissal of substance, of a fundamental identity immanent in difference, is also apparent in several of Stevens' marginal annotations to Charles Mauron's *Aesthetics and Psychology,* the most heavily annotated book in Stevens' extant library.[6] Opposite Mauron's observation that sensibility is produced by "the perception of differences," Stevens notes that "the perception of differences is agreeable in itself." Later he writes, "Originality is an accentuation, through sensibility, of differences perceived."[7] Both of these comments highlight the insistent difference expressed again in Stevens' adage, "The notion of absolutes is relative," which suggests the strictly differential significance not only of

5. *Ibid.,* 56, 65.
6. Stevens' copy is the Kennikat Press edition of 1935, translated from the French by Roger Fry and Katharine John (London, 1935). This text is part of the Huntington Library collection of Stevens papers.
7. The first annotation occurs on p. 45 of Mauron's text and the second on a slip of paper between pp. 48 and 49. Both are quoted in Holly Stevens, *Souvenirs and Prophecies: The Young Wallace Stevens* (New York, 1977), 39, 38.

any particular absolute but also of the very notion of absolutes in general (OP, 158). When we approach Stevens' work with a discourse of difference, our critical attention is drawn to these and other instances of the well-defined indeterminacy and irreducible difference that relativize the apparent naturalness of a critical discourse of identity.

Mauron, like Stevens, was fascinated by the dismissal of substance endorsed by the modern physics of relativity and quantum mechanics, and by the effects that dismissal, with its insistence upon indeterminacy and irreducibly different space-time coordinate systems, must have upon our theories of knowledge and reality. In one of his essays on this subject, "On Reading Einstein" (translated for *The Criterion* by T. S. Eliot), Mauron distinguishes between mystical knowledge and scientific knowledge. The mystic, he says, "holds that any profound knowledge of any reality, implies an intimate fusion of the mind with that reality," and it is this mystical "sense of absolute reality," of a unified identity underlying the differences of phenomenal events that is encouraged by "our everyday habits (and in particular those habits of language in which a substantive designates an object, a thing, as what we call 'real')." The men of science, however, hold that "this mystical knowledge is meaningless, that to try to reach a reality in itself is vain, in as much as our mind can conceive clearly nothing but relations and systems of relations." Where the mystic has a "profound" and, for Mauron, illusory "sense . . . of the reality of things," modern science suggests, against the coercion of its own language, only an irreducibly pluralistic reality of relational differences, so that "wherever this sense of an absolute reality intervenes, this sense of a reality 'in itself,' we must suspect the presence—intrusion, sometimes—of mystical knowledge."[8] Currently, Michel Serres emphasizes the irreducible difference that lies at the center of contemporary physical theories when he writes, "Violence is still—and always—in physics. . . . Beneath the sacred, there is violence. Beneath the object, relations reappear."[9]

Mauron concludes that the "relativist theories . . . are in a direct line of scientific evolution: they are only a stage in the vast process of elimination of things-in-themselves which is going on every day

8. Charles Mauron, "On Reading Einstein," trans. T. S. Eliot, *Criterion,* X (October, 1930), 24–26.

9. Michel Serres, *Hermes: Literature, Science, Philosophy,* ed. Josué V. Harari and David F. Bell (Baltimore, 1982), 124.

in human minds." When Einstein's theories eliminate the absolute immanence of a universal space-time coordinate system, "Time and Space in themselves vanish, to yield place to a multitude of particular systems which have no meaning except in relation to each other," and the classical discourse of immanence is displaced by a discourse of insistent, relational difference. No reality-in-itself underlies this field of differential relationships, and no privileged point of view, one not already involved in and defined differentially by the field, resolves or sums up its plurality; for as Mauron notes, "There is no one observer-elect" whose neutral perspective reduces difference to a determinate, basic "real." As Ilya Prigogine and Isabelle Stengers explain this radically disruptive idea, "We can no longer allow ourselves, as far as the physical world is concerned, the privileged point of view which, when pushed to its limit, we once could have identified as that of God." Reading the texts of modern physics, Mauron finds in them a perspective on difference that makes no appeal to a mystical cognitive core or a difference-resolving reality-in-itself.[10] Neither Stevens nor Eliot ignore this thinking, and these implications of modern physics affect their texts. They must also affect the way we read those texts.

The physicists of the early twentieth century did not pronounce their new theories in a disciplinary vacuum. Einstein's relativity theory in particular was the subject of an extraordinary popularization that found its way into nearly every area of expression, from cartoons to newspaper editorials to films. The physicists had themselves read several philosophers whose texts influenced their own scientific theories. Henri Bergson and William James seem to have been especially important to physicists like Hermann Weyl, Louis de Broglie, and Niels Bohr. And it is these two philosophers whose names appear prominently in Eliot and Stevens. Stevens often alludes to Bergson and James in such essays as "The Figure of the Youth as Virile Poet" and "A Collect of Philosophy." And Eliot knew Bergson and James from his Harvard work in philosophy, and from his time in Paris, and refers to them in (among other places) his 1916 review of Abraham Wolf's *The Philosophy of Nietzsche.*[11]

10. Mauron, "On Reading Einstein," 28; Ilya Prigogine and Isabelle Stengers, "Postface: Dynamics from Leibniz to Lucretius," in Serres, *Hermes*, 147; Mauron, "On Reading Einstein," 30.
11. For an extended discussion of this popularization and the philosophical readings of the physicists, see Carol C. Donley, "Modern Literature and Physics: A Study

Bergson, in describing duration as it operates in mental states—"sensations, feelings, desires, etc."—notes that such states are produced only by irreducible change and difference. "The truth is that we change without ceasing, and that the state itself is nothing but change." He also points out, however, that it is most often "expedient to disregard this uninterrupted change" and imagine that which is "indifferent and unchangeable"—an immanent "*ego*," for example, whose uniform identity can be said to be repeated in difference and change. Such an expediency sounds much like Stevens' statements of convenience or Mauron's observation (through Eliot) that the habits of our language encourage the mystical illusion of absolute reality; each reduces the differences that, thought another way, appear to be fundamentally irreducible. Bergson himself proposes such an immanent substratum to difference, but only to suggest its strictly symbolic or strategic value. "If this colorless substratum is perpetually colored by that which covers it, it is for us, in its indeterminateness, as if it did not exist, since we only perceive what is colored, or, in other words, psychic states. As a matter of fact, this substratum has no reality; it is merely a symbol intended to recall unceasingly to our consciousness the artificial character of the process by which attention places clear-cut states side by side." [12] The symbolic substratum recalls the fundamental differentiating procedure that produces the things (in this case, the psychic states) that are different. For Bergson, nothing precedes this originary difference.

Thus we have the significance of original "perplexity" Bergson cites in his earlier *Introduction to Metaphysics,* in which he distinguishes between opposing schools of thought, the "two metaphysics," on the question of duration. "Some adhere to the point of view of the multiple; they set up as concrete reality the distinct moments of a time which they have reduced to powder; the unity which enables us to call the grains a powder they hold to be much more artificial. Others, on the contrary, set up the unity of duration as concrete reality. They place themselves in the eternal." These metaphysics are incommensurable. Their differences cannot be resolved

of Interrelationships" (Ph.D. dissertation, Kent State University, 1975), 51–89, 92; T. S. Eliot, Review of A. Wolf's *The Philosophy of Nietzsche,* in *International Journal of Ethics,* XXVI (April, 1916), 426–27.

12. Henri Bergson, *Creative Evolution,* trans. Arthur Mitchell (New York, 1911), 2, 4.

or reduced by another more privileged perspective, and Bergson concludes that time, from whichever point of view one holds, appears "as a mixture of two abstractions" that make a difference to each other. Reality profits from this difference, this pattern of interference or perplexity of logic, however, for "as soon as they [the two metaphysics] recover from this perplexity," as soon as difference is immobilized by the privileging of a single metaphysics, "they freeze this flux either into an immense solid sheet, or into an infinity of crystallized needles, always into a *thing* which necessarily partakes of the immobility of a *point of view*."[13] To thaw the *thing*—to dissolve, like a modern physicist, an absolute reality-in-itself and disclose it as the effect of an interference between two incommensurable points of view—is to remobilize difference without appeal to a cognitive core that is other than a symbolic and strategic untying of an original and insistent perplexity. In Serres' discussions of science, such a perplexity, or *clinamen* ("the minimum angle to the laminar flow [that] initiates a turbulence"), originates everything, marking the "moment when an atom in laminar flow deviates from its path, collides with another atom, and initiates the formation of things and ultimately of worlds." Bergson similarly thinks of difference as irreducible, and Prigogine's and Stengers' observation that, with respect to modern science, "things are born where the law is not sufficient to exclude disturbance," describes this insistent component of Bergson's philosophy.[14]

When we read James's *The Principles of Psychology*, we notice a similar dismissal of substantial immanence and an emphasis on differential value. James notes that "no one ever had a simple sensation by itself" and that "when the identical fact recurs, we *must* think of it in a fresh manner, see it under a somewhat different angle, apprehend it in different relations from those in which it last appeared." For James, thought itself consists of the thinking of differential relationships and not of an individualized fact-in-itself, for "the thought by which we cognize it is the thought of it-in-those-relations, a thought suffused with the consciousness of all that dim context." For James, as for Stevens, the physicists, Mauron, Bergson, and, as we shall shortly see, Eliot, it is often convenient not to insist

13. Henri Bergson, *An Introduction to Metaphysics*, trans. T. E. Hulme (New York, 1912), 63.
14. Serres, *Hermes*, 51 n.13, 152.

upon the irreducibility of difference and instead to "formulate . . .
mental facts in an atomistic sort of way." Again it is the habits of
language or the "whole organization of speech" that contributes to
the atomistic thinking of original, different identities underlying
and collapsing the differential relationships that produce them. As
James suggests, "Our psychological vocabulary is wholly inadequate to name the differences that exist," and he supposes that it
must have been easier to avoid atomism in Greek and Latin, for
which, because of their different declensions, "names did not appear . . . inalterable, but changed their shape to suit the context in
which they lay." Thus James concludes that "*a permanently existing
'idea' or 'Vorstellung' which makes its appearance before the foot-
lights of consciousness at periodical intervals* [the presence of a
basic, indifferent immanence represented by and in temporal or spatial difference], *is as mythological an entity as the Jack of Spades.*" [15]
We might say, with Mauron, that such a fundamental identity is a
mystical illusion.

In James's stream of consciousness, then, things or facts emerge
only as repeated sites of an originating disturbance, interference, or
clinamen. James's classic figure of this originary difference is thunder.
"Into the awareness of the thunder itself the awareness of the previous silence creeps and continues; for what we hear when the
thunder crashes is not thunder *pure,* but thunder-breaking-upon-
silence-and-contrasting-with-it." What we hear, in other words, is
an emergent difference only subsequently and figuratively atomized
with the help of language into differentiated things: into silence and
thunder. Much of James's philosophy insists upon the originality of
this difference. "The sense of [the definite image's] relations, near
and remote, the dying echo of whence it came to us, the dawning
sense of whither it is to lead." For James, the "significance, the
value, of the image" is not contained in a permanently existing idea
that it represents. Rather, it emerges within a field of differential relationships, in the "halo or penumbra that surrounds and escorts
it," that cannot be reduced to a central immanence. [16]

James's insistence on original and irreducible difference leads him
to the figure of a pluralistic universe, in which "not only the abso-

15. William James, "The Principles of Psychology," in Richard Ellmann and
Charles Feidelson (eds.), *The Modern Tradition: Backgrounds of Modern Literature*
(New York, 1965), 715, 716, 720.
    16. *Ibid.,* 718, 723.

lute is its own other, but the simplest bits of immediate experience are their own other," and to the conclusion that the "minimal fact" of experience is the mark of difference. Experience exists only as a node of difference, for "sensational experiences *are* their 'own others' . . . both internally and externally." The "gist of the matter," James says, "is always the same": the eternal return of difference and of a field of differential relationships irreducible to a central, self-identical cognitive core. "Something ever goes indissolubly with something else. You cannot separate the same from its other, except by abandoning the real altogether and taking to the conceptual system." The Jamesian *real* is a reiteration of the same that insistently resounds with difference, and "nature is but a name" for this excess of difference that "overflows its own definition" and cannot be held to the "closed equations" of the conceptually "self-identical." [17]

The center of experience, the essence immanent in all differences, is for James a figure with only pragmatic or strategic significance. No sun of immanence arises in the Jamesian text without the self-eclipsing mark of difference, for "the fact is all shades and no boundaries." No privileged center reduces an insistently pluralistic universe to a basic core of identity, for such a center emerges only within a differential relationship with a marginal other that displaces it. James perceives the "continuity of experience," then, not as the movement of an essence in difference, but as a chain of repeated ruptures, displacements, interferences, and decenterings. As the physicists suggest, the privileged point of view from which this chain can be summed up—an observer-elect immune to the de-centering process that must displace him—can only be a mystical or methodological illusion. From any point of view, from any provisional, conceptual center, "something always escapes" resolution, "something else is self-governed and absent and unreduced to unity," and it is this insistently irreducible difference that the pluralism of James's universe suggests. [18]

The connections between James's pragmatism and Eliot's dissertation on F. H. Bradley have recently been traced in an excellent article by Walter Benn Michaels. For Michaels, "Eliot's pragmatism does not consist in any simple repudiation of the ultimate although

17. William James, *A Pluralistic Universe* (Cambridge, Mass., 1977), 127, 128, 129.
18. *Ibid.*, 130, 145.

it generally begins with the denial that certain seemingly fundamental distinctions (between the given and the constructed, for example, or the real and the ideal) have any ultimate justification." Rather, Michaels finds Eliot suggesting that "the fact that we can adduce no ultimate justification for such distinctions does not mean that they are in any sense 'invalid.' They have their 'practical' significance; they are only local and unstable but they are real." This emphasis on the strictly local and practical nature of significance recalls Stevens' "statements of convenience" and Planck's "working hypothesis." As Michaels summarizes Eliot's argument on perception, "A true perception cannot be distinguished from a false one by virtue of its proximity to an object but only by virtue of its consistency with a 'world.'" Similarly, in a statement that echoes the well-defined indeterminacy Stevens finds central to physics and the strictly methodological significance of Mauron's observer-elect, Michaels observes that, according to Eliot, "there can be no method, no rules for generating correct interpretations, since interpretations, correct and incorrect, are always and only local, a function of the situation you happen to be in." For Eliot, "facts are not, in the realist sense, given; they are produced by . . . a 'system'" or by an ineluctably non-neutral, situational point of view. The conditions of that point of view are, according to Harold Joachim, unexpressed and yet implied, and are acknowledged by Eliot to be "irreducible." What Michaels emphasizes about Eliot's pragmatism is the understanding of facts, of the universally and immanently real or basic, as "determined by local 'conditions' whose 'transcendence' involves not their theoretical absorption into a higher whole but what might instead be called a lateral movement from one set of local conditions to another," with each locality being "in no way more self-conscious, no more able to be reflective about its subjectivity" than any other.[19]

Michaels observes that Eliot's "account of the constitutive nature of points of view [and his "focusing on the way in which one point of view can make a difference to another"] does not lead to a vision of the universe as consisting of parallel points of view, parallel worlds, which, because they never interact, can make no difference to one another." Such a categorizing vision immobilizes difference in, to use Stevens' phrase, "the folds of the garments of the

19. Walter Benn Michaels, "Philosophy in Kinkanja: Eliot's Pragmatism," in Samuel Weber and Henry Sussman (eds.), *Glyph 8* (Baltimore, 1981), 174, 180, 185, 186, 193, 194, 188.

ghost . . . of Aristotle." But, as Michaels points out, this is not the
vision of Eliot's dissertation, for such worlds do overlap, and it is
only in their interference that, like Jamesian "sensational experiences," these methodological worlds differentially *are*. Michaels
concludes that "Eliot's pragmatism is not the link which joins the
relative with the absolute; it is instead a way of understanding the
identity of relative and absolute and denying them both."[20] This
way of thinking insistently remobilizes difference as the differentiating process that produces the differences fundamental and necessary to these relative and local worlds.

The preceding passages suggest that the texts of Eliot and Stevens
emerge as notable points within an interdisciplinary matrix of texts
that emphasize an insistent thinking of difference. Such texts influence our readings of the poets by producing disturbances in the
canonically New Critical understandings of both Eliot's incarnational rhetoric and Stevens' Adamic language. With them in mind,
our readings of these two prominent figures of American poetry
must undergo a type of Kuhnian paradigm shift. Indeed, such a shift
has occurred in the past ten years or so, since the critical acceptance
of such continental thinkers as Jacques Derrida, Michel Foucault,
and Serres.[21] We can no longer work in a critical world where meanings are secure and stable, where continuity lies just beneath all ruptures and indeterminacies, or where a neutral and determining presence—God, man, or the critic himself—stands as the referent that
resolves and closes the differences traced by poetry's metaphoric detours. The discourse of difference we have been describing interferes
insistently with such a critical world, shifting its certainties into
newly redeployed problems which then become available for scru-
tiny. It begins with the affirmation of the productive difference we
have, in our repeated appeals to immanence, until lately sought to
reduce and overcome.

   Difference intervenes most insistently when Eliot's and Stevens'
writings turn to questions of signs, tropes, and representations, and
it is this intervention that the following chapters trace. Where we
disclose each poet's repeated appeals to in-different immanence—
to, in Eliot, a still point or, in Stevens, a supreme fiction or center—

20. *Ibid.*, 197, 200.
21. Thomas S. Kuhn, *The Structure of Scientific Revolutions* (Chicago, 1962),
149 and throughout.

there we will also notice an interference or disturbance that re-mobilizes difference and marks these points as sites of a problem. These interferences of difference with in-different identity, of representation with presence, or of trope with literality (and vice versa) can be said to produce the texts of Eliot and Stevens in the same way that physics suggests that different things are produced by the *clinamen* of an originating declination, or information theory suggests that messages are the products of their differential relationship with random noise. We shall not say, however, that Eliot, in his employment of a highly Christianized rhetoric, is blind to these interferences, or that Stevens, with his playful circulation of fictions, insightfully sets right the error of Eliot's orthodoxy. Rather, besides reciting the differences between the two discourses and the ways in which each deploys difference, this book seeks to affirm the energizing differential process that repeatedly and productively resonates within each differential siting.

One
Eliot, Peirce, and Signs

T. S. Eliot's 1916 Harvard dissertation takes knowledge and experience in the philosophy of F. H. Bradley as its central subject and thereby places itself squarely within a tradition of epistemological inquiry; however, a seemingly more peripheral topic of investigation shadows Eliot's discussions. This topic, an elaboration of a certain interpretation of signs and symbols, sometimes moves to the center of Eliot's philosophical discourse but for the most part it is confined to the fringes. Most readings of the dissertation assume that Eliot's marginal discussions of semiotics are controlled by his central philosophy and that the semiology can be understood, in other words, as an elaboration of the philosophy.[1]

And yet the semiology to which Eliot's dissertation frequently returns complicates such readings by disturbing the epistemological and phenomenological theories they explore. Indeed, Eliot's semiology affects any logically coherent theory, for it is the logic of philosophy, the unified *logos* of philosophical knowledge, with which it interferes. His meditations on signs and symbols cannot simply be

1. See especially J. Hillis Miller, *Poets of Reality: Six Twentieth-Century Writers* (New York, 1974), 130–80, Anne C. Bolgan, "The Philosophy of F. H. Bradley and the Mind and Art of T. S. Eliot: An Introduction," in S. P. Rosenbaum (ed.), *English Literature and British Philosophy* (Chicago, 1971), 265, and Lewis Freed, *T. S. Eliot: The Critic as Philosopher* (West Lafayette, 1979), xii.

read as a subtext contained by the Bradleian philosophy. Rather, the philosophy emerges only along with the problematic semiology that interrupts it. This interference is central to the dissertation, for Eliot's marginal meditations on signs and symbols erupt in and radically disturb its central philosophy, and it is to this insistent interruption that a reading to which the semiology makes no difference would be blind.[2] An exploration of this marginal interference must take place, not in the philosophy of Bradley, but in the semiotics of Charles Sanders Peirce.

Eliot knew well Peirce's work on logic, phenomenology, and semiotics, and he refers to it at a crucial moment of the dissertation: "I mean . . . by symbol both what Mr. Peirce calls by that name and what he calls an eicon; excluding the index" (KE, 103). Peirce's general theory of signs is central to Eliot's discussion, and the specific reference here is to that essay in *Elements of Logic* entitled "The Icon, Index, and Symbol." In it, Peirce expands upon his definition of the sign, or *representamen*. For Peirce, "a sign . . . it is something which stands to somebody for something in some respect or capacity. It addresses somebody, that is, creates in the mind of that person an equivalent sign, or perhaps a more developed sign. That sign which it creates I call the *interpretant* of the first sign. The sign stands for something, its *object* . . . the *ground* of the representamen." A symbol is a type of sign particularly tied to speech and writing. "All words, sentences, books, and other conventional signs are Symbols" that, as signs, determine their replicas, or interpretants.[3] Still based in an object, a symbol by convention controls the interpreting sign it produces.

This proliferative nature of the sign (or symbol) constitutes its being a sign as such. To be itself, the sign must be replicated by an interpretant that, as another sign, is necessarily different from it. The original sign exists only in this differential relationship with another sign, for "no Representamen actually functions as such until it actually determines an Interpretant." Because of its fundamentally relational nature, the sign sets off a differential chain of signification that is presumably closed at its origin, the in-different object. And yet, as Peirce points out, the presence of the object is not essential to the functioning of the chain of significations, for the

2. Miller, *Poets of Reality*, 131.

3. Charles Hartshorne and Paul Weiss (eds.), *Collected Papers of Charles Sanders Peirce* (8 vols.; Cambridge, Mass., 1960), II, 135, 165.

"Representative Quality [of the representamen] is not necessarily dependent . . . upon its actually having an Object."[4] For Peirce, it is the relationship between representamen and interpretant that is central; the relational field of significations need not have an original object at its center.

But even presuming the presence of an object, the status of the ground in Peirce's semiotics remains far from certain. He indicates that an object may without difficulty become simply another sign within a representational space, or a sign representing itself as an object. Thus the ground of the signifying chain can never be securely fixed, for it is always interfered with by its different potential as another sign. This is a critical aspect of Peirce's semiotics, in which "mere presentment," the presence of a present object, "may be a sign." He observes elsewhere that "the idea of *manifestation* is the idea of a sign," thus suggesting that where the object appears, where the grounding origin of the chain of significations presents itself, there the sign originally intervenes. Jacques Derrida observes about Peirce's semiotics that "from the moment that there is meaning there are nothing but signs." In the rhetoric of phenomenology, then, the "conception of being . . . plainly has no content," but rather has only referential significance as a sign in an irreducibly differential field of significations. When the sunflowers of the parable with which Peirce opens "The Icon, Index, and Symbol" turn toward their solar object or referent, they trope the sun not as the "pinpoint source of truth" but rather as a sign representing the proliferation of signs in this differential field.[5] Since metaphor is, for Peirce, that which depicts the "representative character of a representamen," the sun marks the centrality of the relationship of representation and not a transcendental ground to which this relationship makes no difference.

Thus for Peirce the sign's perfection is seen not in its ideal adequation to an object, but rather in its prolific production of other signs. The sign becomes an interpretant that in turn becomes another sign, and so on *ad infinitum;* and "if the series of successive interpretants comes to an end, the sign is thereby rendered imperfect." The endless series of representations can be thought of as

4. *Ibid.*, II, 157.
5. *Ibid.*, II, 136, 156, 176–77; Jacques Derrida, *Of Grammatology*, trans. Gayatri Chakravorty Spivak (Baltimore, 1976), 50; Hartshorne and Weiss (eds.), *Collected Papers*, I, 288; Jacques Derrida, "White Mythology: Metaphor in the Text of Philosophy," *New Literary History*, VI (Spring, 1975), 44.

closed only through an obscuring conceptualization in which a representation is conceived as the truth. But this subreptitious truth itself emerges only in a relationship with the "irrelevant" that cloaks it, and thus a maneuver to end the differential chain of representations also redeploys it.[6]

When Eliot refers in the dissertation to signs or symbols, he has in mind Peirce's sense of symbols and icons, but not his sense of index. This exclusion is provocative because it points toward Eliot's emphasis upon the differential aspect of Peirce's semiotics and opens the dissertation to a reading that insists upon difference without appeal to a unique cognitive identity or a unified immediate experience. For Peirce, icons, indexes, and symbols form a second trichotomy of signs defined by their relationship to their referential objects. An icon "is a sign which refers to the Object that it denotes merely by virtue of characters of its own, and which it possesses, just the same, whether any such Object exists or not."[7] No original object need ever be present for this type of sign to function as such, as thus the icon deploys a chain of interreferential significations to which the presence or absence of an object makes no difference.

A symbol, in this Peircean trichotomy, "is a sign which refers to the Object that it denotes by virtue of a law, usually an association of general ideas, which operates to cause the Symbol to be interpreted as referring to that Object."[8] Like the icon, the symbol is originally unmotivated, in that it bears no natural or essential relationship to the object to which it is understood to refer. Unlike the icon, however, the interreferentiality of the symbol is artificially subjugated to a law or hermeneutical paradigm that, like the subreptitious conception of truth, appears to dismiss irrelevant differences from the symbol and to cause it to be interpreted in only one way, in terms of a single, grounding object. But the very necessity of the law interferes with its operation, for it marks the strictly methodological and strategic nature of the particular referential relationship it prescribes. In this interference and therefore in the law itself can be seen the differential life of the sign. For Eliot, letters and writing begin where the hermeneutical law is not strong enough to suppress such interferences. "I am tempted . . . to regard as a dead letter a law which cannot be violated" (KE, 131). Thus both the

6. Hartshorne and Weiss (eds.), *Collected Papers,* II, 169; I, 171.
7. *Ibid.,* II, 143.
8. *Ibid.*

icon and the symbol are for Peirce signs that can function in a differential field of signification without the identity of an object, and both are reflected in Eliot's term *symbol*.

Peirce's index, however, is a sign "which refers to the Object. . . . It necessarily has some Quality in common with the Object, and it is in respect to these that it refers to the Object." Whereas the icon and the symbol acquire their significance in a differential relationship with other signs, the index appears to be a sign whose significance is determined by an object that must itself exist, for it is seen to be causally connected to its referential object, to be affected by it, and to share common properties with it. Removed from the horizon of Peirce's semiotics, the indexical sign seems to represent a type of natural signification in which signifying sign and signified object are originally and unbreakably united, in which the difference that constitutes the index points only to the higher identity of the object itself. It is precisely this understanding of the sign's referentiality as naturally oriented toward a determining object that Eliot forcefully excludes from the dissertation. This exclusion marks Eliot's rejection of an understanding of signs as simple representations and his insistence upon the strictly differential nature of signs as they emerge in an interreferential field of significations. In Eliot's dissertation, signs refer to and interpret other signs, and it is only in this interreferential relationship that all signs are originally constituted.

For Peirce, the space of signs is completely illimitable. One cannot isolate a transcendent truth of logic or philosophy from the strictly differential interreferentiality of significations. Signs do not serve either truth or logic as its expression or representation. Rather, the logic of truth is never other than a local and convenient conceptualization or interpretation of signs, since "the warp and woof of all thought and science is the life [Eliot's differential life that interferes with any methodological law] inherent in symbols." Logic is thus, for Peirce, "only another name for *semiotics* . . . the quasi-necessary, or formal, doctrine of signs." It is, in other words, "the philosophy of representation." As Derrida observes about Peirce, "Semiotics no longer depends on logic," but logic and the truth it purports to reveal is primordially a semiotic, in the same way that *being* in Stevens depends differentially upon *seeming*.[9] Object, meaning, truth, phenomenon, being—all elements of logic and phi-

9. *Ibid.*, I, 129; II, 134; I, 184. Derrida, *Of Grammatology*, 48.

losophy, all names for *logos*—emerge originally as signs in an illimitably differential field of significations. Hermeneutical methodologies seek to immobilize the differential life of signs through the application of a supplemental law of interpretation; or as Peirce writes, "The scientific and philosophical worlds are invested with pedants and pedagogues who are continually endeavoring to set up a sort of magistrature over thoughts and other symbols." However, such a mastering reduction of difference can be accomplished only symbolically—only, that is, in a rhetorical maneuver that itself remobilizes difference.[10]

Whereas Peirce's semiotics begins with the differential relationship between a sign and its problematic object, Eliot in the dissertation begins with what he calls "immediate experience" or "feeling," a grounding origin for the field of signs and symbols that shows itself to be no less problematic than Peirce's. Quoting Bradley, Eliot writes that feeling is "the immediate unity of a finite psychical centre" and that it exists "before distinctions and relations have been developed." Defined as a center of unity out of which the differences of history emerge, feeling appears as a timeless, primordial identity in which subject and object are one and that, since it supports time itself, has no history. For Bradley, immediate experience "is not a stage which shows itself at the beginning and then disappears, but it remains at the bottom throughout as fundamental." Not simply an origin that the differences of time and history leave behind, immediate experience (feeling) appears rather as the bottom that underlies and unifies temporal differences. Eliot reflects this idealist thinking seventeen years later in the conclusion to *The Use of Poetry and the Use of Criticism,* where he writes that poetry "may make us from time to time a little more aware of the deeper, unnamed feelings which form the substratum [we hear in this term echoes of the Bergsonian substratum] of our being, to which we rarely penetrate; for our lives are mostly a constant evasion of ourselves, and an evasion of the visible and sensible world" (KE, 16, 22; UPUC, 155).

This theme of a fundamentally unified substratum that stands under the evasions or declinations of time is deployed early in Eliot's dissertation. But like Bergson's substratum, Eliot's "unnamed feelings" emerge only to be interfered with, in the same way that Peirce

10. Hartshorne and Weiss (eds.), *Collected Papers,* II, 129.

deploys his "grounding object" only in a relationship with the disruptive possibility that it may be another sign in the illimitable chain of significations and therefore no transcendental ground at all. In Peirce, "mere presentment" is another name for a sign; in Eliot, feeling turns out to be never simply itself. "We do not find feeling without thought, or presentation without reflection." In fact, feeling or immediate experience, which purportedly names a substratum of unity, can in no way be distinguished from an "ideal construction," for "the line between the experience, or the given, and the constructed can nowhere be clearly drawn." Where Peirce's object marks within itself an essential difference, Eliot's feeling or immediate experience discloses a similar perplexity in which the constructed cannot be separated from the given, or the reflection from the presentation. Immediate experience, in other words, insistently interferes with itself as the sign of mediation, since "in order that it should be feeling at all, it must be conscious, but so far as it is conscious it ceases to be merely feeling." Although Eliot refers to feeling as the unified substratum that stands under all differential relationships, he also points out that "without these relations, which give the feeling its whatness, the feeling could not be said to exist." Its "whatness" is its difference from itself, an insistent, constituting, and irreducible difference which guarantees that "immediate experience . . . is not as such present either any*where* or to any*one*" (KE, 17, 18, 20, 23, 31).

Eliot agrees with Gottfried Benn's assessment of poetic origins. "There is first, [Benn] says, an inert embryo or 'creative germ' . . . and, on the other hand, the Language, the resources of the words at the poet's command. He has something germinating in him for which he must find words; but he cannot know what words he wants until he has found the words; he cannot identify this embryo until it has been transformed into an arrangement of the right words in the right order. When you have words for it, the 'thing' for which the words had to be found had disappeared, replaced by a poem." For Benn, the poem replaces the "embryo" in the same way that, for Eliot, the words defining an experience substitute for the original experience. But like Peirce's self-interfering object, Eliot's experience may be words, for "the original experience may have been itself a definition." The beginning and ground of Peirce's semiotics is always the site of a constituting interference that is both obscured and redeployed by a supplementary and subreptitious law. Similarly, in

Eliot's dissertation, one begins only with an illusionary pseudo-beginning. "You start, or pretend to start, from experience . . . and build your theory" (OPP, 106; KE, 167). Theory begins not with a unified experience, but with a deployment of difference, with an interference that constitutes differentially both the experience and its complementary words, both the ground and its evasive reflection. Theory starts, for Eliot, at such a site of difference.

Other redeployments of the differentially constituted field of significations are found in the key terms *idea, concept,* and *thing.* For example, Eliot, reflecting Bradley, observes that the idea is a " 'concrete habit or tendency,' a 'selective rule,' and again it is a thing . . . which stands for something else." Like feeling, the idea functions only within a problematic referential relationship: it refers both to itself and to something else. The idea is, in Saussurian terms, a signified that always signifies something else, and it is this interference that for Eliot constitutes the idea as such, since "it is not true . . . to say that an idea has an object, for idea *is* (not *has*) a reference to an object." What the idea refers to is the concept, and in this inter-referential relationship both idea and concept are constituted. "The pointing of the ideas at the concept constitutes the reality of the concept." But the concept, the figure indicated by the idea, does not close the chain of significations, for it is itself another reference. Although the concept can be interpreted to be a "real" that cannot be properly represented by a signifying idea, it nevertheless is "present and practical" only as it is "used to *stand for* a . . . group of ideas" (KE 43, 93, 40). The concept stands for the idea in an interreferentiality in which each is constituted only as a difference from and reference to the other, that is, in a differential relationship that recalls a Peircean infinite regression of signification.

Thus both idea and concept are constituted only as sites of difference in a fundamentally differential field. A thing also reflects this insistent internal difference that constitutes it. "The thing, in order to be a thing even, must be capable of entering into a kind of existence in which it is not a thing." The thing itself is never simply an identity, for its "kind of existence" takes place only in a relationship with something that interferes with it. The appearance of the thing is therefore the sign of this constituting relationship—an originating and differential relationship that disturbs the very notion of original identity or simplicity. This movement by which unity is constituted is, for Eliot, the very definition of a sign. "A sign has its existence beside its content, and it is just this separate existence—the fact that the sign might be misinterpreted or simply not recognized as a sign at all, which makes it a sign." The sign is both faithful representation and erroneous misrepresentation, and this essential interference both "makes it a sign" and puts at risk a difference-constraining content. Indeed, it is only in the sign's essential declination from such a content that it is a sign at all, and thus to suggest, as Eliot does, that every "idea is a sign" is "a most treacherous statement," since it asserts that every idea appears within a constituting relationship with the essential noise of difference that disturbs its identity (KE, 99–100, 48).

A complication also appears in what Eliot calls the "dangerous problem of error." Like the sign's treacherous and essential heterogeneity, error can never be excluded or confined to a particular location, but is rather the difference that emerges in every contextual site. Error cannot be confined, for example, to the margins of a discourse, but may take its place at that discourse's very center. But, then, if error were discovered at the center of a discourse, could this discourse be discarded as treacherously flawed, and error thus be finally delimited? Eliot concludes that it cannot, since all truth emerges only in a differential relationship with error. "You never can tell at precisely what point . . . mistake occurred; how much that is to say was received unaltered from without and how much was constructed from within." The boundary between the mistaken inference and the true can never be firmly and finally drawn, for one always interferes with and cannot be excluded from the other. This interference produces for Eliot an impasse rectified only locally "in a practical world," with an "essentially *practical* solution," and not in a "metaphysically . . . real world" (KE, 52, 160, 117). For Eliot, error marks the irreducible interference within every true statement and thus articulates the differential relationship in which both truth and error, the unaltered and the constructed, are constituted.

When Eliot discusses poetry, he often focuses on the problem of error and accident. In "The Social Function of Poetry," he observes that "poetry, like every other single element in that mysterious social personality which we call our 'culture,' must be dependent upon a great many circumstances which are beyond its control." What poetry is by intention can thus never be distinguished from what poetry is by accident. This interreference between intention and accident is essential to literature and cannot be delimited, for "every single work in [our literature] may be defective in something. This may be a necessary defect, a defect without which some quality present would be lacking: but we must see it as a defect, at the same time we see it as a necessity" (OPP, 13, 71). This treacherous and essential heterogeneity is central to literary discourse and cannot be seen as simply befalling a pure intentionality from some corrupted outside.

Error is thus a dangerous problem for philosophy because it blurs the line between philosophic and literary discourse's intentional truth and its unmotivated and accidental "defect." Indeed, error dislocates all such dualities, undermining in its essential homelessness all simple oppositions. The interference of error is central to both Peirce's and Eliot's semiotics, in which it marks the essential heterogeneity of the sign. In Eliot's dissertation and criticism, this difference that resists methodological constraint often appears in the figure of an unaccountable fringe or interference within the discourse itself. When Eliot writes of feeling as a site of difference, he refers to it as a fringe, taking its place only on the discourse's margins. Similarly, in his essay titled "Poetry and Drama," he describes the interrupting other at the center of prose drama. "It seems to me that beyond the nameable, classifiable emotions and motives of our conscious life when directed towards action—the part of life which prose drama is wholly adequate to express—there is a fringe of indefinite extent, of feeling which we can only detect, so to speak, out of the corner of the eye and can never completely focus." Poetry, like drama, is also a site of this interference, for "poetry is a constant reminder of all the things that can only be said in one language, and are untranslatable" (OPP, 93, 13). Each of these discourses is thus characterized by interferences of the unsaid with the said, the unaccountable with the accountable, the indeterminate accident with the determinate intention—the interference, that is, of meaningless noise with the message that seeks to exclude it from itself. But in Eliot the excluded noise always returns to inhabit and interfere with the message, and it is only with this interference that the discourse is ever constituted.

By emphasizing the essential heterogeneity of signs and discourses, Eliot negates figures of a unified, central referent upon which the interreferentiality of signs can close. For example, he discusses the character of Becky as an "imaginary object" in *Vanity Fair* and notes that although "Becky exists as an event in the life of

Thackeray, and as an event in the life of every reader . . . the object denoted by the word Becky does not exist, for it is simply the identical reference of several points of view." Becky's name denotes an interreferential field of interpretations not reducible to a core of identity. These local points of view are incommensurable, but their identical reference produces a central identity (Becky) that names an imaginary object marking only the point of interference between them. In a similar discussion Eliot writes that, in general, a "statement has meaning only so far as we refer [any two statements] to a single world, in which we vaguely feel that they are reconciled by experience; they are held together, that is, by a feeling of their *identical reference*, though that to which they refer does not exist" (KE, 126, 110–11). The feeling that holds these different statements together does not suggest a transcendent, referential identity. Rather, it again marks the interference point between the statements, a site of difference constituting the differential meaning of both statements. The identical reference of two incommensurable statements is thus to the constituting difference between them, or to the difference each makes in the other. Meaning names the site of the redeployment of this difference.

The centrality of difference and interference is addressed by Peirce in his book on phenomenology. Discussing action and perception, he notes that the "idea of other . . . becomes a very pivot of thought." He extends this theme to reality itself, observing that reality is not a presence as such but rather "is that which insists upon forcing its way to recognition as something *other* than the mind's creation." [11] Thought and reality, subject and object, thus rely, like the Eliotic sign, upon a constituting interference, an insistent and internal pivot that interrupts the identity of both subject and object as the necessary condition for their appearance. At several points in the dissertation Eliot touches upon this originating difference that fractures the simple identity of experience. Like a sign, which constitutes and is constituted by an illimitably differential field of interreference without cognitive core, experience marks a site of difference. Never a simple unity, it emerges only differentially, for "no experience is self-consistent" (KE, 148–49, 28).

Thus when Eliot observes that "in the growth and construction of the world we live in, there is no one stage, and no one aspect,

11. *Ibid.*, I, 162, 163.

which you can take as the foundation," he suggests that there are an indefinite number of foundations from which to choose. He also speaks of the impossibility of any foundation to be simply itself, since it is marked by difference on the inside and constituted differentially (with respect to the other foundations or points of view) on the outside. Difference does not accidentally befall unity but is rather the constituting characteristic of any discursive, cognitive, or phenomenal world. It is the interference within metaphysical thought that, in spite of Eliot's disclaimer that "differentiation in what should be simple will fall outside of our metaphysics," nevertheless inhabits it completely (KE, 151, 36).

The theory of signs that emerges from Eliot's dissertation disturbs not only the metaphysics of simple identity but also the understanding of language as the re-presentation of a unified and determinate essence. Like signs, names in Eliot mark the impossibility of naming properly and thus repeat a constituting difference. The name "denotes our object which is not itself, and yet, when we ask just what this object is which is denoted, we have nothing to point to but the name." The object named is similarly the site of a difference that interferes with the illusion of simple self-presence. "We . . . have an object which is constituted by the denoting, though what we denote has an existence as an object only because it is also not an object." The illimitable homelessness of error, which blurs the line between intention and accident, thus occurs in another form in denotation, since "in the use of any phrase we cannot always be sure to what extent we are meaning the denotation or meaning the meaning, and how far we are denoting the denotation or denoting the meaning." Although the phrase is intended to denote or name a meaning, meaning is never simply present. "The speaker can only mean; and even if he means his own 'state of consciousness' what is really active is a meaning which is not meant" (KE, 134, 137, 127, 93). Where meaning appears, it does so only along with the interference of accident and error. Denotation in Eliot is thus the mark of unfilterable noise.

Eliot later notes that "a substantive in complete isolation does not exist" and thus underscores language's differential character. The closure or orientation of this differential field can be delineated only through a supplemental meaning that would function like the law associated with Peirce's icon. Eliot quotes Bertrand Russell that "we must attach *some* meaning to the words we use, if we are to speak significantly and not utter mere noise." As the above argument has suggested, however, words always interfere with such a supplemental law of meaning by denoting both meaning and noise in their originally differential relationship. This noise resists the control of a law of meaning while being a constituting part of the meaning/noise relation, and thus there can be no context in which noise is not present. In "The Frontiers of Criticism," Eliot writes, "I am even prepared to suggest that there is, in all great poetry, something which must remain unaccountable however complete our knowledge of the poet, and that that is what matters most" (KE, 132, 104; OPP, 124).

The insistent difference that runs through Eliot's theory of signs complicates what appears, at other places in his writings, to be a desire to banish noise and to close language and signification upon a determinate identity of meaning. Eliot warns in the dissertation that "it is essential to the doctrine which I have sketched that the symbol or sign be not arbitrarily amputated from the object which it symbolizes." The image of amputation presumes a natural, organic relationship between symbol and object symbolized, a relationship severely questioned by Eliot's other discussions of signs. And yet this relationship later becomes a prime criterion in Eliot's criticism for judging the health of a discourse. In the early essay, "Swinburne as Poet," Eliot writes that "language in a healthy state presents the object, is so close to the object that the two are identified." The health of identity, of a discourse from which noise and difference have been excluded, is underscored in "Four Elizabethan Dramatists" by the idea of the homogeneous self-consistency of art: "It is essential that a work of art should be self-consistent, that an artist should consciously or unconsciously draw a circle beyond which he does not trespass." Eliot later applauds Ben Jonson for just such a staying within the lines: his writing "is the careful, precise filling in of a strong and simple outline, and at no point does it overflow the outline." To overflow the outline is to interrupt the healthy identity between the discourse's surface and depth, between signs and meaning. Such dislocation is the target of Eliot's attack on Milton. Unlike Shakespeare or Dante, in whose discourse there is "no interruption between the surface . . . and the core," Milton employs the rhetorical style in which "a dislocation takes place . . . so that the inner meaning is separated from the surface, and tends to become something occult" (KE, 132; SW, 149; SE, 93, 130; OPP, 163, 162). Rhetoric, with its dislocations and interruptions, here appears to be a sickness infecting language's naturally healthy body and interfering with the identity that is the sign of that health.

And yet the interpretation of identity as a sign of health is disturbed in the dissertation by a contrary understanding of identity as a sign of disease. Eliot points out that memory is not the recollection of "the object as in itself it really is, but [of] its image." Memory always takes place in the realm of signs, which repeat an essential heterogeneity with any object. Identity between sign and object is here marked as disease. "The effort of memory . . . would be to identify itself with the past experience, and the completion of the process would be hallucination . . . [which] is not the satisfaction and consummation of memory, but its disease." This malady is avoided by memory's redeployment of an illimitable chain of signification in which meaning itself is always interfered with. Meaning is not present at the moment of speech; rather, it is supplemented into the remembered speech by memory (KE, 49, 50). And yet, as Peirce points out and Eliot reiterates, "The warp and woof of all thought . . . is symbols."[12] Thus memory is itself another moment of language, a type of speech that in turn defers meaning again. Memory is in this manner a differentiating process that, by deferring meaning, interrupts the hallucinatory identity between sign and object, an identity Eliot speaks of elsewhere as the health of discourse. In an image that Wallace Stevens similarly employs in "Notes toward a Supreme Fiction," Eliot writes of this identity as a "mystic marriage" whose site of consummation is "not exactly determinable": as, that is, a union that must always suffer interruption and dislocation and that can be celebrated only as an incessantly redeployed problem—as the insistently problematic return of difference (KE, 135).

The desire for the sign's mystic marriage to a nonrhetorical object—and the interference that unsettles that marriage—is particularly apparent in Eliot's strategies in *Murder in the Cathedral*, a play in which Eliot the dissertation philosopher conflicts with Eliot the theologian-playwright, whose project is to reduce to insignificance the differences between the historical interpretations of Becket's

12. *Ibid.*, I, 129.

death. These interpretations appear to be incommensurable, and it is this perplexity that Eliot would have his play resolve by shifting its emphasis from a temporal understanding of signs and history to what William Spanos has defined as a sacramental understanding. As Spanos points out, this latter understanding proposes a universe in which "all objects in space (nature) and all events in time (history) are placed according to a universal scheme and given transcendent significance"—in which, in other words, spatial and temporal differences are controlled by the identity of a "transcendent significance" they represent. It is through the notion of *figura* that this sacramental understanding, characteristic of modern Christian verse drama, interprets history, so that "history itself becomes a *figura*, concrete yet figurative; in short, symbolic." In this fashion, the sacramental perspective reads in the signs of history a mystic marriage of "time and eternity, the many and the one, motion and stillness . . . concrete reality and value."[13]

Figural interpretation is most completely analyzed by Eric Auerbach in his chapter on *figura* in *Scenes from the Drama of European Literature*. He defines history as a differential field of interreferential events. "Figural prophecy implies the interpretation of one worldly event through another; the first signifies the second, the second fulfills the first. Both remain historical events; yet both, looked at in this way, have something provisional and incomplete about them; they point to one another and both point to something in the future, something still to come, which will be the actual, real, and definitive event." The structure of this field recalls the incommensurable interpretations or identical references Eliot describes in his discussion of *Vanity Fair*. For Auerbach, historical signs similarly remain "provisional and incomplete," since they both point toward and defer the definitive, transcendent event. Rather than revealing a transcendent referent, the signs instead insure that a final real event will remain forever veiled by a falsifying figure. They point to this event by marking their divergence from it; hence the event can never "appear" as such, but it can be distinguished only as an unknowable term that the figure always obscures. For this reason, history is not an "eternal present" but is rather "forever a figure," a Peircean infinite regression of signs in which no transcendent significance, no nonrhetorical object or presence, is discernible. Its

13. William V. Spanos, *The Christian Tradition in Modern British Verse Drama: The Poetics of Sacramental Time* (New Brunswick, 1967), 50, 29, 50.

interference with transcendent identity is in fact the constituting condition of history itself, an idea implicit in Auerbach's observation that when history is fulfilled, *figura* will pass away. In the terminology of Eliot's dissertation, history or *figura* becomes a dead letter if it is identified with the *natura* interpreted as its law; if it does not, that is, insist upon its essential heterogeneity. Thus figural interpretation, which seeks to resolve the differences of history in a transcendent unity of significance, itself engenders difference by necessarily deferring this real event and thereby continually redeploying history as a differential field of interpretations. The resolution of these differing interpretations can be accomplished only with the intervention of a spiritual act of faith, which, like a "practical solution" to an infinite regression of signs, adds another interpretation (*i.e.*, another figure) to an already saturated field (KE, 117).[14]

The essential heterogeneity of historical signs interferes with the sacramental vision with which Eliot, in his play, seeks to intervene in history's differences. As E. Martin Browne points out, Eliot's drama is an attempt to "celebrate the cult associated with a sacred spot by displaying the story of its origin."[15] In order to display this origin, Eliot must deal with a historical event, the death of Thomas Becket. Several earlier writers, most notably Tennyson and George Darley, wrote of this event from an essentially historical point of view, but it is precisely this perspective that poses a problem for Eliot. As the Knights' speeches at the end of Part Two suggest, Becket's death, when seen from a strictly historical perspective, has been overinterpreted and has produced incommensurable interpretations that influence each other but are not controlled by a central, resolving meaning. The Knights, for example, offer three conflicting interpretations of the event. For the Second Knight, the murder was necessary to subordinate the Church to the State. For the Fourth Knight, Becket's death was not a murder but was instead a "Suicide while of Unsound Mind." And for the Third Knight, it was merely the natural result of the play of historical forces. Murder, suicide, or natural consequence—these interpretations of Becket's demise are incommensurable and no observer-elect appears to resolve their differences. As Becket himself suggests, every historical event repeats

14. Eric Auerbach, *Scenes from the Drama of European Literature* (New York, 1959), 58, 53–54.

15. E. Martin Browne, *The Making of T. S. Eliot's Plays* (Cambridge, England, 1969), 37.

this irreducible difference: "For every life and every act / Consequences of good and evil can be shown" (MC, 84, 78–80, 73). At the
close of the first part, he explains that, from a historical perspective,
his death will produce a proliferation of different interpretations.

> . . . I know
> What yet remains to show you of my history
> Will seem to most of you at best futility,
> Senseless self-slaughter of a lunatic,
> Arrogant passion of a fanatic. (MC, 45)

It is in this proliferation of incommensurable interpretations that
Eliot seeks to intervene with a rectifying sacramental hermeneutics.
By displaying the authentic origin of the cult, his project is to marry
this differential field of temporal interpretations to the identity of a
sacramental figure.

Becket is himself no less a sign of essential heterogeneity than is
his death. *Murder in the Cathedral* can in fact be read as a struggle
over the right of any single law (barons, Church, King) to restrict
Becket's significance and actions. As the play begins, the Second
Priest expects that Becket's return will restore to Canterbury its authentic father, the reconciling personage who

> . . . shall be at our head, dispelling dismay and doubt.
> He will tell us what we are to do, he will give us
>   our orders, instruct us.
> . . . .
> . . . when the Archbishop returns
> Our doubts are dispelled. (MC, 17–18)

But as it continues, the play marks this personage as the site of a
dangerous interference. According to the Three Knights, Becket is
the "archbishop who was made by the King; / whom he set in [his]
place to carry out his command" and who must therefore transact
the king's business in his absence. Becket, in other words, is here
seen as an instrument of the King's law. But as the Three Knights
also point out, Becket is "in revolt against the King," and this revolt
is figured by his assumption of an additional signification, one that
interferes with the King's law and resists his authority. Although
he was "made by the King," Becket in Part Two presents himself as
the instrument of Church law. "It is not Becket who pronounces
doom, / But the Law of Christ's Church, the judgement of Rome"
(MC, 59, 63, 65). Thus Becket appears in the play as an essentially

heterogeneous figure, and it is the interference of two incommensurable interpretations of this figure—as the sign of the Church and as the sign of the King—that constitutes the drama's action.

Eliot's purpose is to banish the noise of incommensurable historical interpretations from the pure sacramental message of Becket's death, and this purpose is most apparent in the play's implicit rejection of the Knights' rationalizations and in Becket's explicit refutation of the first three Tempters. These figures not only tempt Becket with the good time of youth, with temporal power, and with treachery against the King, but more important, as Spanos has pointed out, they "orient Thomas' vision in the direction of the past, the present, and the future, that is, on the level of time." By rejecting them, Becket rejects "historical time or the world in its three temporal manifestations," a gesture that marks Eliot's displacement of purely temporal interpretations of Becket's story.[16] This displacement enables Eliot to intervene in the incommensurable historical accounts of Becket's death, which rely upon the various interpretations of the eyewitnesses, with texts from other sources, and it results in a "novel and peculiarly unhistorical treatment of the protagonist's character."[17] This intervention marks the interference of Eliot the theologian, who seeks, in an appeal to a sacramental perspective, to make insignificant the historical differences between incommensurable points of view, with Eliot the philosopher, whose dissertation insisted upon such essential differences. By means of this intervention, Eliot intends to render completely meaningful "the empty land / which is no land [the field of incommensurable interpretations], only emptiness, absence, the Void" (MC, 71).

For this reason, the play shifts its emphasis away from the historical moment of Becket's death and onto the moment in Part One when he avoids the "greatest treason" of the "last temptation" ("To do the right deed for the wrong reason") and presumably places his will in line with the divine will. It is this moment, in which Becket decides to allow the right deed to happen for the right reason, that is the origin of the cult of Canterbury that Eliot seeks to display, for it is by this decision and not simply by his death (which produces the noise of incommensurable interpretations) that Becket qualifies

16. Denis Donoghue, *The Third Voice: Modern British and American Verse Drama* (Princeton, 1959), 85; Spanos, *Christian Tradition*, 83, 84.

17. Grover Smith, Jr., *T. S. Eliot's Poetry and Plays: A Study in Sources and Meaning* (Chicago, 1950), 183.

himself for sainthood. This is, for Eliot, the moment that rectifies historical differences by pointing to their law, to the Word-made-Flesh that is their transcendent significance. But as Hugh Kenner points out, this moment of the "purification of Becket's will," which is the "main moral action of the play," is insufficiently analyzed.[18] Kenner understates the problem here, for this transcendent law of history cannot be dramatized as completely authoritative, as entirely free from the noise its invocation is designed to exclude. The play displays it here only as a silence (Becket's silence) over which the Chorus, the Tempters, and the Priests speak their various interpretations. When this moment finally breaks into speech—when Becket returns to the stage and exclaims, "Now is my way clear, now is the meaning plain"—that speech interrupts the silence it explains (MC, 44). Becket's historical present disturbs the transcendent atemporality of the silent law; his interpreting *now*, always belated, designates the *then* of the moment with which it can never coincide. Thus history's law emerges in history either as a muteness about which there is no information or as a significance already marked by the interfering noise of interpretation.

The silence of the authoritative moment locks it outside of history and protects it from history's perplexing interruptions. Outside of time, however, history's law makes no difference to temporal history. As Becket himself observes, "It is not in time that my death shall be known" (MC, 74). For there to be any information at all about history's transcendent significance, its law must be supplied with a historical event like Becket's death, which appears as its figure (where there is information, there must also be the *figura*). But this event deploys a field of incommensurable interpretations over which no law exercises final control, in which there are only differing and unrectifiable points of view. The necessary *figura* opens this interreferential and essentially heterogeneous field in which different interpretations are constituted only insofar as they interfere with and dislocate the identity of a transcendent significance that must therefore forever remain a problem.

History is constituted by this declinational relationship with atemporal transcendence, the *clinamen* of time and the timeless Eliot elsewhere names Incarnation. The Chorus is the figure of this declination. In Part One it explicitly defines itself as a figure that

18. Hugh Kenner, *The Invisible Poet: T. S. Eliot* (New York, 1959), 280.

must bear witness to the impending catastrophe in the cathedral. It awaits the return of Becket the father, who as the lord of Canterbury will be the rock providing a "firm foothold / Against the perpetual wash of tides of balance of forces of barons and landholders," the turning world that is the temporal life of the Chorus. But for the Chorus this resolution spells death, for it will bring a "doom on the house, a doom on yourself, a doom on the world." As a historical figure, the Chorus lives only through an essential heterogeneity with its law. It therefore seeks to displace Becket and urges him to return to France, to "set the white sail" between itself as figure and Becket as law (MC, 11, 17–18, 19, 21). It is the Chorus that, in this play, insists upon the difference Eliot the theologian seeks to render insignificant.

Like the Chorus, the play itself deploys difference insistently, for its two parts are constructed around an interruption, or Interlude. This moment of rhetoric (Becket's sermon) stands between the atemporal moment of Becket's decision, unable to be dramatized, in Part One and the belated drama of historical interpretations in Part Two. The interlude is the pivot of the play, the point of differentiation that constitutes both parts by holding them apart and enforcing their essential heterogeneity. In other words, it interrupts the mystic marriage of the two parts, of history and transcendent significance, and prevents the collapse of temporal differences into atemporal silence and in-difference. Its intervention thus engenders both transcendent law and historical interpretations, and marks the differential relationship—an Incarnation, not as the re-presentation of an essence, but as an essential difference—apart from which neither has any meaning.

The interference between Eliot the dissertation philosopher, whose semiology insists upon the differences essential to a differentially constituted field of signification, and Eliot the theologian, who desires the closure of this historical field upon an identity of transcendent significance, is itself the perplexity that designates *Murder in the Cathedral* as the interreference of two incommensurable points of view. Neither the semiologist nor the theologian controls this perplexity, for each point of view bears on the other, and thus each emerges only within this differential relationship. Like the Incarnation, the *clinamen* in which time and the timeless are deployed differentially, *Murder in the Cathedral* is the site of hermeneutical difference, whose peaceful denouement occurs only as another practical solution to difference that is itself difference's redeployment, a "fiction which unravels" as it is woven (MC, 85). Although Eliot the theologian seeks to banish the dissertation semiologist's point of view from his first major religious drama, his desire cannot successfully exclude the interrupting noise from the purely Christian message. Instead, it marks the inevitable return of the noise of difference and repeats that essential heterogeneity as the constituting condition of history, of signs, and of the play itself.

The Eliot of *Murder in the Cathedral* exhibits an anxiety about difference not immediately apparent in the dissertation, where difference is affirmed as a productive process and identity is described as disease. In *Murder*, and in Eliot's other texts stressing a sacramental hermeneutics, the story of difference is often obscured by an incessant desire for identity. Difference is seen as a problem in need of a solution, an aberration from which Eliot seeks relief through an appeal to the identity of God. The words that insistently deploy difference in the dissertation Eliot later seeks to regather into the transcendent unity of the divine word. From the perspective of Eliot's sacramental hermeneutics, difference expresses this transcendent identity.

But from the semiological perspective of the dissertation, signs lead only to more signs in a chain without a containing object; difference engenders more difference in a field of dynamic interrelationships between words not circumscribed by the unity of a divine Word or cognitive core. This is the Peircean influence on the dissertation, and it is a perspective that intrudes upon the sacramental hermeneutics of identity. The semiological and the sacramental, difference and identity, interfere with each other in Eliot; as incommensurable points of view they emerge differentially, and it is their tensive balance that can be read in his poetry.

This balance can also be read in Stevens, where the story of difference and identity, words and the Word, is told in a different register. Where Eliot's sacramental hermeneutics seeks relief from difference, Stevens' poetry looks for ways to thwart the entropic, homogenizing influence of the specter of identity or the ghostly unity of a cognitive core. Whitehead, Bradley, and Peirce are a relief from Plato, Aristotle, Kant, and Hegel, whom Stevens, in a letter to Theodore Weiss, terms "divinities of the Styx" (LWS, 476). The mystic marriage of sign to object, difference to identity, desired in Eliot's sacramental hermeneutics but denied in his semiology, is repeated by Stevens as the affirmation of the differential relationships in which all words and all things originally emerge.

But Stevens' affirmation is itself never pure and simple, for it too can be read only along with its disruptive complement, the "ancient cycle of desire" of which "Notes toward a Supreme Fiction" gives an account. Difference and identity, affirmation and desire, emerge within this cycle as interferences to each other, the interferences redeployed by poetry as its constituting condition. Stevens exhibits very little of the anxiety of Eliot the theologian, but his story is much the same, for the ancient cycle of desire is the insistent story of poetry.

Two
Representation and Difference

The problem of signs that plays marginally in Eliot's dissertation also appears throughout Stevens' varied meditations on reality and the imagination. His continual return to the theme of the fiction, supreme or otherwise, repeats a questioning of signs that becomes more pronounced in the later portion of his poetic career. In this repeated questioning, Stevens often insists upon the irreducibly differential character of signs, sounding much like Eliot in his dissertation. The poems collected in *Transport to Summer*, for example, often speculate upon the nature of poetic language and, in turn, upon the signs that compose it. The centerpiece of the volume, "Notes toward a Supreme Fiction," deploys signs and representations as sites of some perplexing problems: What is the relationship of signs and representations to being and presence, of signs to time and change? What are the characteristics of pleasure, and how is this pleasure connected to the emergence of signs? What, for Stevens, constitutes a sign, and how do signs function in writing? Like Eliot's dissertation, whose Bradleian philosophy is continually interrupted by its Peircean semiotics, Stevens' "Notes," like many of his other poems, reads like a speculative commentary upon itself as an "invented world" of signs.

This speculation is most insistent in a poem Stevens wrote three years after "Notes," "Description Without Place." Both poems begin by considering what "Notes" calls the "inconceivable idea of the sun," with "Description" providing what is virtually a reading of the first section of "Notes." The opening line of "Description"— "It is possible that to seem—it is to be"—focuses on the status of signs and representations by outlining a certain relationship between *being* and *seeming,* key terms that recall a classical, hierarchical theory of signs as representations of essence or being (CP, 380, 339). In its probing of this relationship, "Description" repeats the problem that in Eliot's dissertation appeared as the question of the substratum of immediate experience and of the connection between a differentially constituted field of significations and a methodological law of transcendent significance. For Stevens, the productive and constituting relationship between being and seeming is exemplified by the sun, which, as an example, functions metonymically. In the *Rhetoric,* Aristotle suggests that examples are metonymical comparisons in which two propositions or historical events emerge differentially. Each is an example of the other in an interreferential relationship that cannot be generalized into simple identity. Although both events deal with the same subject (invasion, in Aristotle's first example), both retain their particularity and historical difference.[1] The interreferentiality of examples reflects the differential relationship also characteristic of Eliot's figural interpretation of history in *Murder in the Cathedral.* To say that the sun is an example, then, is to sketch the relationship of the sun to that which it exemplifies as a resemblance that insists upon difference—a resemblance in which the *as if* of *seeming* cannot be completely identified with the *is* of *being.*

This relationship, then, disturbs an understanding of signs as classically hierarchical representations of a signified presence, as, in other words, seemings that, through the detour of their signification, refer to and bring to light a signified being in whose presence the difference between presence and representation can be overlooked. Here Stevens takes a habitual figure for such presence (the sun) and interferes with its significance in a gesture repeating the similar interference that characterizes both Peirce's use of the sun and Eliot's deployment of immediate experience. The sun emerges as a sign of the seeming that is an essentially differential relationship

1. *Rhetoric and Poetics of Aristotle,* trans. W. Rhys Roberts and Ingram Bywater (New York, 1954), 133.

constituting the being of all things. The sun, then, like Eliot's immediate experience and Peirce's object, does not simply signify the end of difference, but rather it marks the site at which difference is redeployed productively in a field of things that exist only as they interreferentially affect each other.

Stevens' opening proposition has two important implications. First, all things are seemings, or signs, making the world fundamentally semiological in character. And second, these things are constituted only as sites of difference in a nonhierarchic semiological field of differential relationships without an essential core of identity. Such a field reflects the most radical conclusion of Saussure's investigations into the semiology of language—namely, that "in language there are only differences *without positive terms*." But where Saussure's conclusion continues to posit a core of substance representable by signs, Stevens' proposition intervenes in all such ideas of substance with an insistent difference.[2] The substance of the sign appears to be only the difference it makes to another sign. Thus for Stevens the sign must be characterized not as a container in which the substance of meaning is either present or absent, but rather as the trace of this differential relationship.

Thus in "Description" what powers this semiological world is not a transcendent identity of meaning but rather a differential force figured by the exemplary sun and, later in the canto, by the queen whose influence produces the sun as a sign. Like the sun, this queen emerges as a sign of seeming and, therefore, as a nominal center, like Eliot's practical solution, of the differential field of significations. She makes the sun *seem* "By the illustrious nothing of her name," which fills the "golden vacancy" of the solar semé with an identity of content; but she herself "seems to be on the saying of her name." Like that of the sign she produces and whose significance she determines, her being is differentially constituted as both the determining referent of the sun and the "illustrious nothing," both herself and not herself, both signified and signifier. Her name repeats, in other words, the differential relationships in which both being and seeming originally and irreducibly emerge. By elaborating upon its opening proposition—which, as a possibility, both "is and . . . / is not and, therefore, is" the trace of the difference that is

2. Ferdinand de Saussure, *Course in General Linguistics*, trans. Wade Baskin, ed. Charles Bally *et al.* (New York, 1959), 120.

its being—this canto describes an indelibly semiological world in which being is not only the sign of the end of signification but also as the redeployment of the signifying chain ("Her time becomes again, as it became / The crown . . . of her fame"), the sign of its eternal return (CP, 440).[3]

To speak, then, of being as the substratum of seeming, as a transcendent substratum not already a part of a semiological field, is to overlook the differential relationship, the metaphoricalness or *as if* of seeming that both constitutes being and interferes with its identity. Ignoring this relationship collapses this difference into a homogeneous essence that, as the second canto finally insists, nevertheless remains "merely a thing that seems / In the seeming of an original in the eye." Nietzsche's observation that ideas arise only through "an arbitrary omission [later, through "forgetting"] of . . . differences" shadows this passage, as does Eliot's statement that the "idea *is* . . . a reference" (KE, 95).[4] Stevens' line from "The Pure Good of Theory"—"It is never the thing but the version of the thing"—is also relevant here (CP, 332). There is never identity without the trace of difference, never the "solid block" without the interference of the stylized, signifying "manner." Just as being emerges only in a differential relationship with seeming—or, for Eliot, the sacramental message is constituted only differentially with the interfering noise of interpretation—so even sensual phenomena in Stevens are themselves semiological in character, since all phenomena (what we "see, / Hear, feel and know") are "actual seemings." Peirce's observation that logic is "only another name for *semiotics*" could here be reiterated as Stevens' suggestion that phenomenology is only another name for semiology.[5] The essentially signlike character of all things, however, produces for Stevens the subtlety of apparition, the elusive density of phenomena (as opposed to the in-difference of "flat appearance"—but there is even interference here, since this flatness is subtly interrupted by "delicate clinkings not explained") that emerges, not because the signs of appearance represent a transcendent substratum of being, but because the being of signs is irreducibly differential.

3. The similarity to the semiology of Peirce is striking. In LWS, 476, Stevens writes, "I have always been curious about Pierce [*sic*]."
4. Geoffrey Clive (ed.), *The Philosophy of Nietzsche* (New York, 1965), 507.
5. Charles Hartshorne and Paul Weiss (eds.), *Collected Papers of Charles Sanders Peirce* (8 vols.; Cambridge, Mass., 1960), II, 134.

Thus when "Notes" sketches the "idea / Of this invention, this invented world" of poetry and signs, it begins, like Peirce's semiotics and Eliot's philosophy, with a caution against understanding this idea as the product of an originating identity.

> Never suppose an inventing mind as source
> Of this idea nor for that mind compose
> A voluminous master folded in his fire. (CP, 381)

Rather, the idea must be perceived as a site of pure difference, as something inconceivable that can never be identified. "Description" suggests that this insistent difference, which traces in all our images their status as exiles expelled from a heavenly home, sets in motion the semiological invention. But as "Description" also implies, this expulsion (the "fall" of signs away from an originating identity) never could have taken place, since in Stevens' semiological world everything begins with difference. As "Notes" states, "The death of one god is the death of all," and this death both prospectively and retrospectively interferes with the interpretation of the semiological world as hierarchical and representational, as originating in and re-presenting an essential identity. Like the figure of the inconceivable idea, "Phoebus was / A name for something that never could be named," and thus it emerges as a metaphor of original exile and difference. A conception that does not conceive, a name that does not name—traced here is the constituting difference repeated by every image in the invented world. The "project for the sun" is to look forward to the perplexity traced by both the sun and the queen in "Description."

> . . . The sun
> Must bear no name, gold flourisher, but be
> In the difficulty of what it is to be. (CP, 381)

The "difficulty of what it is to be" is to be differentially, to be that which affects something else, to be both named "gold flourisher" and that which "must bear no name." The sun, the practical center of this invented world, does not name an essential core around which the semiological field turns; rather, it redeploys the essential differences by which that field is originally constituted.

The perpetual exile of signs, the insistent difference "Notes II" calls "the celestial ennui of apartments," keeps reopening the invented world by renewing its differential force, by reinscribing in the semiological system practical figures of original identity that, like the sun, redeploy the difference fatal to the self-identity of truth itself. The "first idea" thus marks the productive life of the invented world as this interference of identity with difference, of, for example, being with seeming, of the named with the unnameable, or, to recall Eliot's figure of Incarnation, of the timeless with time. This interference traces a continual displacement that renews the differential life of our exiled images. There is only, for Stevens, the "ennui of the first idea," the "ancient cycle" in which the priest and the philosopher desire an end to the differential exile of signs only to reiterate that exile in the knowledge that what they have "is what is not," in a return of difference that is again the beginning of desire.

Stevens' "ancient cycle of desire" adequately describes Eliot's theological project in *Murder in the Cathedral*—to resolve the differential life of historical signs and interpretations in a unified truth not subject to the interruptions of temporal interpretations. But obscured by that play's project is the inevitable result of such desire. In "Notes," the desire for truth pure and simple illuminates the essential difference it seeks to overcome, for "not to have is the beginning of desire." Perceived difference elicits the desire that discloses difference, and in this perpetual displacement, in the appearance of truth only along with its ravishment or interference, is reflected the ancient cycle of exile that refreshes the life of the sign. As Stevens writes elsewhere, "Life consists / Of propositions about life" that are never other than eccentric and that therefore speak of a proliferation of local, metaphorical truths with no rectifying or central core of truth itself (CP, 355–56).

The poem, in other words, springs not from a representable, referential origin or even from a fall from such an origin, but rather, to use a phrase from Eliot's dissertation, from an essential heterogeneity Stevens characterizes as primordial exile, a place of signs and images that are the traces of this constituting difference. The "first idea," therefore, "the quick / Of this invention," is not the idea of the sign or image as re-presentation, not, that is, "to shape the clouds / In imitation" either of a divine source, a heaven, or of ourselves projected into that heaven as the natural source or shaper of the invented world. Thus

> . . . Adam
> In Eden was the father of Descartes
> And Eve made air the mirror of herself, (CP, 383)

and all three "found themselves / In heaven as in a glass," romantically projecting themselves as the constituting origin of a semiological world they felt reflected their "inventing mind." But "The first idea was not our own," and therefore not the myth of reflection and representation repeated in the Eden story. Rather the clouds, the signs the representational myth presumes are shaped in imitation of man, preceded us, and "We are the mimics" of this "muddy centre." As the being traced in "Description Without Place" suggested, the idea of man is itself a product of the differential *quick* of seeming. The "myth before the myth began" redeploys a "venerable and articulate and complete" language that cannot be reduced to an originating identity.

The air into which Eve projects herself as inventing mind thus figures the signs and images of poetry, not as a mirror, not as a medium reflecting or expressing an originary self, but as a "bare board," an open space to which our "Abysmal instruments"—of writing, perhaps?—supplement the "sweeping meanings that we add." This open space of signification, however, is not simply a *tabula rasa;* as a "Coulisse," it is already a site of difference and bears the "bright-dark" traces of other poems, theatrical scenes, and supplementary meanings. The semiological world therefore appears neither as the mirror of self-presence (as Eve, Adam, or Descartes would have it) nor as the bare board of absence (over which we can write a truly original fiction of meaning), but as a coulisselike structure, a palimpsest of differences in which the irreducible interference of the "eccentric" with a "muddy centre" is the differential base repeated by every design of meaning (CP, 151). Stevens' invented world of language thus both rewrites and effaces the myth of the inventing mind as the originating source of meaning.

Signs, then, do not begin in a paradise of meaning or intentionality; they begin differentially in the original displacement of exile, never arriving at or representing a core of meaning that is not eccentrically supplementary. The question that opens the eighth canto of "Notes,"

> Can we compose a castle-fortress-home,
> Even with the help of Viollet-le-Duc,
> And set the MacCullough there as major man? (CP, 387)

alludes to just this supplementation and considers the possibility of redeeming the exile of signs by rebuilding representation (a project like Eliot's in *Murder in the Cathedral,* but here aided by the arch-restorer, Viollet-le-Duc) as the home of a determinate core of identity (the MacCullough). The MacCullough is this canto's figure of the transcendent truth itself, whose appearance may end the exile of signs by summing up (and thereby controlling) their perpetual eccentricities. He figures the "Beau linguist" whose speech controls noise and difference, for he is "a form to speak the word / And every latent double in the word." But as Stevens explains in a letter to Hi Simons, "MacCullough is any name, any man," and as the canto suggests, "the MacCullough is [simply] MacCullough" (LWS, 434). Thus this figure of transcendence is deployed as an arbitrary expedient, a supplementary beginning or home for the invented world, composed as the strictly local and methodological starting point and restored to language's differential field only as a belated supplement—only, that is, as the sign of an artificial and arbitrary identity whose control over difference is interrupted by the very expediency of its composition. The story of "MacCullough himself . . . lounging by the sea" is the tale of the return of noise and of the "latent double in the word." Here MacCullough, composed to be the transcendent identity represented by the differential field of significations,

> . . . might take habit, whether from wave or phrase
>
> Or power of the wave, or deepened speech,
> Or a leaner being moving in on him,
> Or greater aptitude and apprehension. (CP, 387)

Latent in MacCullough, in other words, is another, different being from which he himself might "take habit" as a sign. MacCullough's identity is also the sign of the essential difference whose redeployment displaces any such expediency and reconstitutes the exiled, differential life of the sign. The *as if* of *seeming,* like the *as if* in which the waves "at last were never broken," collapses to the unity of transcendent identity only through the mediation of a practical, expedient fiction, only, that is, within the "crystal hypothesis" that is another redeployment of the *as if* of *seeming.*

These supplemental meanings, variously called truth, being, logos, essence, presence, are, as both "Description Without Place" and the second canto of "Notes" suggest, the expedient, privileged metaphors of philosophy and poetry that can be read as names for a core of truth at which the Peircean infinite regression of signs ends. Interpreting the metaphors in this way, however, again discloses the impasse or difference that both constitutes them and interferes with their identity. Their significance, then, is strictly methodological; they differentiate the field of significations into a central core and an eccentric periphery. Through the repetition of this methodological supplementation, Stevens' invention—a differential field of significations that has no essential core of transcendent significance—works, and its working produces an illimitable proliferation of local truths. The later Eliot often seeks to muffle the noise of this methodological work, but in Stevens one can always hear the delicately clinking mechanism that produces meanings and truths. This figure of the semiological invention as a productive machine is suggested in as early a poem as "Like Decorations in a Nigger Cemetery," which proposes that

> The chrysanthemums' astringent fragrance comes
> Each year to disguise the clanking mechanism
> Of machine within machine within machine. (CP, 157)

Here the trope of the natural almost silences the mechanism that produces it. In a much later poem, "Repetitions of a Young Captain," the theatrical *real* chugs along "like a machine left running, and running down" until it is broken up and displaced by "the spectacle of a new reality," by a new universe that is nevertheless another theatrical production, since this displacement repeatedly substitutes one theater for another and never a natural truth for the machine-made drama of methodology (CP, 306, 309).

Everything in Stevens "ticks like a clock" as part of the differential machine of words and signs. Even the truths this semiological machine produces emerge only as sites of difference, for they are not entirely the result of an authorial intention or an inventing mind. Rather, as the seventh canto of "Notes" suggests, such truths are strictly incidental; they are "not balances / That we achieve but balances that happen" (CP, 157, 386). Where such meaningful balances occur, there is the site of a propitious accident that both produces truth and negates its natural or intentional significance. In Stevens, truths never acquire universal value or validity; they are rather the local accidents repeatedly produced by the workings of the machine of language. Such truths inevitably depend

> . . . on a walk around a lake,
>
> A composing as the body tires, a stop
> To see hepatica, a stop to watch
> A definition growing certain and
>
> A wait within that certainty, a rest
> In the swags of pine-trees bordering the lake. (CP, 386)

These Stevensian truths, like the Nietzschean "mobile army of metaphors," thus emerge only along with the noise of unintentional accident, in the same way that poetry, in Eliot's "The Social Function of Poetry," must be "dependent upon a great many circumstances which are beyond its control" (OPP, 13).[6] The productive working of Stevens' machine of language presupposes the lack of transcendent, universal significance, the absence of an inventing mind, and the essential heterogeneity of signs. Its deficiency constitutes its productive life as a mechanical "Swiss perfection," whose *schwarmerei* is in Stevens a familiar music.

This *schwarmerei* is sounded again in the ninth canto of "Notes," which turns on the difference between the "idiom" of apotheosis and the mechanical "click-clack" of reason's "applied / Enflashings." This difference is profound. The phrases aligned with the idiom of apotheosis figure the sensual body of language, the particular sounds of its words repeated as rhetorical performance—"the romantic intoning, the declaimed clairvoyance")—while the "click-clack" of reason appears as the source of the "major abstraction" named "major man." The difference is between the concrete and the abstract, the particular and the general, the body of the sign and the bodiless signified. What this canto traces, in a restatement of Canto I's "project for the sun," is the effect this supplemental abstraction has on the idiom of the sign. It is applied to the signifier in the same way that Canto IV's generalizing "sweeping meanings" were added to the clouds of representation. It functions only as a point of reference always "evaded in the mind," as a generalized law of reason never strong enough to suppress the sign's particular, idiomatic declination, and this evasive difference is redeployed with every appeal to such an abstract generalization.

The history of the "major abstraction," of the generalized truths discoverable in the meanderings of language, is thus in Stevens always the story of the foundling, of the homeless figure whose gene-

6. Clive (ed.), *The Philosophy of Nietzsche*, 508, 510.

alogy and authority remains an unresolvable problem. It is the story, in other words, of the illimitable proliferation of signs and of their interreferentiality. The interdict that ends this canto is a startling reversal of Canto I's myth of the expulsion of imagery from transcendent meaning, and it produces not a unifying resolution, but a reconstitution of the problem of difference. Here, Stevens advises us to "look not at [the foundling's] colored eyes. Give him / No names. Dismiss him from your images." The image itself expels the accident of meaning. The interdict that dismisses the supplement insists upon the difference between one image and another, thus marking a methodological strategy in which the difference that originally constitutes Stevens' semiological world is redeployed. Stevens emphasizes the "flor-abundant force" of differentiation that is the "happy fecundity" of this invention.

The final canto of "It Must Be Abstract" plainly propounds this differential force, the fecund principle in which all things are constituted. The "major abstraction" deployed in Canto IX as the expedient referent from which all our images differentiate themselves is both the exception to the invented world of those images and "part / Though heroic part, of the commonal." This sign is a site of difference that, as the interference of the exceptional and the common, of the image and the expedient referent, constitutes the productive difference the other nine cantos of "It Must Be Abstract" characterize as the force powering the semiological machine. The difference that eternally returns in the ancient cycle of desire—we recall, from Canto II, that "not to have is the beginning of desire"— is characterized here as the process of reading "figures."

What rabbi, grown furious with human wish

· ·

Does not see these separate figures one by one,
And yet see only one, in his old coat,
His slouching pantaloons, beyond the town,

Looking for what was, where it used to be? (CP, 389)

Desire, the "human wish" for the resolution of composition and difference in the identity of a transcendent truth, is another name for reading or interpretation, for the collapsing of the poem's "separate figures" into the exceptional "only one." But as in *Murder in the Cathedral*, in which Eliot desired to close the field of incommensurable interpretations upon an identity of transcendent signifi-

cance, this reading produces only another MacCullough, foundling, exemplary sun, or homeless tramp—only, that is, another
belated supplement that, in "looking for what was, where it used to
be," repeats the originating difference that is the "flor-abundant
force" of the semiological world. Only in the repetitions of this difference and in the search that redeploys it is the future possible,
both as the future of signs and, as "Description Without Place" proposes, as the future itself, since being is nothing other than the differential being of signs. The "ancient cycle" of desire opens that future by tracing in it the energizing force of difference out of which it
emerges. "Like Decorations in a Nigger Cemetery" reflects the difference disclosed by the search.

> If ever the search for a tranquil belief should end,
> The future might stop emerging out of the past,
> Out of what is full of us; yet the search
> And the future emerging out of us seem to be one. (CP, 151)

It is of this invigorating difference that Stevens advises the ephebe
to "confect / The final elegance." Because difference cannot be reduced to an identity that would be final, his advice can only be a call
to continue the exile and project of the refreshing search.

Thus what is traced in the first section of "Notes" and in the later
"Description Without Place" is a theory of signs that describes the
semiological world as an interreferential field, thus distinguishing
itself from a theory of representation. The fifth canto of "Description" turns on two of the issues critical to the project "Notes" outlines: the strictly differential character and significance of signs, and
the supplementation—the productive proliferation of signs—that
perpetually defers the collapse of difference into the identity of representation. Experience, whether it is phenomenal experience (the
"actual seemings" of a summer's day) or the reading of a text (the
"potential seemings . . . on the youngest poet's page"), is always in
Stevens, like immediate experience in Eliot, interfered with by signs.
No experience can therefore be self-consistent, for all experience
exists only referentially with respect to something else, to a "knowledge incognito" that is itself constituted as a point of interference or
disguise. At the center of both phenomenal experience and cognitive knowledge lies the difference between two disguises or signs,
between the Old Testament "column in the desert" and the New
Testament "dove" that alights on it as its interpretant. Both column

and dove emerge as figural and interreferential signs whose existence depends only on each other and not upon the presence of a transcendent significance that homogenizes their historical and textual differences. The column and the dove figure the proliferation of signs that begin in the difference of exile and end in another redeployment of difference.[7]

Nevertheless, "Description is / Composed of a sight indifferent to the eye" and therefore suggests a theory of representation that distinguishes between a world of sensory phenomena and the descriptions that, fundamentally, have no bearing on it—between, that is, being as transcendent identity and seeming as its re-presentation. But as Stevens goes on to modify this definition, description also suggests

> . . . an expectation, a desire,
> A palm that rises up beyond the sea,
>
> A little different from reality:
> The difference that we make in what we see
>
> And our memorials of that difference. (CP, 344)

The indifferent ontological phenomenon was earlier called the "seeming of an original in the eye" and here is marked as the site of the "difference that we make in what we see." It therefore cannot be simply reduced to a sight that excludes the difference-making process of seeing. Seeing makes a difference (there is never a neutral observer-elect), and it is only in this differential relationship that the things that are different—sight and eye, object and subject, perception and perceiver, reality and imagination—are originally constituted. Description repeats this constituting difference in which identity emerges only as the product of a differentiating and intervening point of view. For Stevens, the difference repeated by seeing and seeming marks the insistently differential being of all phenomena, of all things. It is this essential difference, like that emphasized by Eliot's dissertation, that his "world of words" redeploys (CP, 345).

The "chronologies" in the first canto of Stevens' "It Must Change" tell a history without rupture, a seamless, continuous movement of the present in which "this changes and that changes." In one of these chronologies, "the bees came booming as if they had never

7. Hartshorne and Weiss (eds.), *Collected Papers*, II, 169.

gone / As if hyacinths had never gone." Here the language of being overlooks the disruptive *as if* of seeming that interrupts the continuity of "this" and "that" with the interference of difference. However, in the invented world that Stevens introduces to the ephebe, there are no "changing essences," since identity, or being, is essentially differential. Thus a history of this world must trace not the continuity of identity but the repetitions of this constituting difference. Like the theater of the real in "Repetitions of a Young Captain," the discourse of chronology and being, of the continuity of essences that change only to repeat their identity, appears as a rhetorical "machine left running, and running down." But in Stevens' poetry, change makes an irruptive difference, for the repeated cycle of supplementation involves the violent displacement of one scene by another, one theater by another, one sign by another, in a reiteration not of this or that but of the sustaining process of difference. The irruptive change marked by the return of the *as if*—"The bees came booming / As if—The pigeons clatter in the air"—interferes with the bluntness of identity and the discourse of being, displacing its unity with subtleties of analogy and difference and disclosing identity as "merely a thing that seems" (CP, 389, 397, 306, 340).

The difference here is between a rhetoric of the continuity of being, of the resuming of identity in change and difference, and an irruptive, energetic beginning in a displacing differentiation. Such a beginning is always a beginning *again*, a reiteration of the pretense of original beginning and a renewal of the irruptive force of difference "It Must Be Abstract" characterized as the exile (another figure of a beginning in displacement) that is the sustaining quick of the semiological world. *Resuming* implies the continuity of a representational structure centered on the original identity of "inexhaustible being"—a continuity in which the difference between signifier and signified (the *as if* of analogy and metonymy) is ultimately overcome in a recapture of one by the other. For Stevens, language and writing do not begin in representation ("the first idea was not to shape the clouds / In imitation") but in the irruptive, discontinuous, and unclosable difference traced as an originating force powering the field of significations. Thus in Stevens all beginnings and origins are marked by the trace of the other, of repetition, of "Again, the diva-dame," of the nonidentical iteration (in time) or difference (in space) only within which do the things of the invented world emerge (CP, 353).

The rhetoric of metaphysics, then, is characterized by generalization, by the collapse of the "bright particulars" that emerge in time from an ongoing differential force into a monumental figure of identity, an immortal being that is seen as transcending time and its differences. Such Apollonian generalization, in Nietzsche's terms, ignores difference and, for Stevens, reconstructs the rigid suspension and permanence represented by such spatial monuments as the "great statue of General du Puy" (CP, 344, 391). This monument suggests the difference-collapsing continuity between past and present figured in the preceding canto of "Notes" by the return of "inexhaustible being." The general, at least for the lawyers and doctors who come to the Place du Puy to study the past, lives on in his representation, in the monument that stands as a sign of the continuity of history. As a figure of permanence and a sign of immortality, the monument translates the differing particulars of time into a spatial form. But this statue is for Stevens not simply characteristic of "our more vestigial states of mind." It also marks the difference that interferes with its monumental identity. The monument is, on one hand, the representation that immortalizes the general, the essential origin of the monumental sign. But on the other hand, it discloses the impossibility of such an origin, for "there never had been, never could be, such / A man." The monument, in other words, represents the origin—the particular sign refers to a generalized meaning—only as that which it could never have had. Thus the monument to the closure of signs is itself the site of reiterated interference and difference. Housed in the statue is neither the living presence of the general nor the remains (the dead body) of his absence but, since the "neighboring catafalques / Bore off the residents of its noble Place," rather the traces of his original plurality. The different local particulars memorialized in the Place du Puy do not collapse to a homogenized, universal generalization, since the general is himself originally multiple. Thus the monument obscures difference in its hierarchical, pyramidal form—in, that is, the metaphysical portrayal that "was rubbish in the end."

Such monumental generalizations are characteristic of the various stories of origin found in "Notes toward a Supreme Fiction"—stories that, like Eliot's in *Murder in the Cathedral*, purport to trace the dispersed differences of time back to a single, original source. The story of the fall of our images from the cleanliness of a remote heaven is one such tale of origin that the first canto of "Notes" interferes with, and two other similar tales are recited in the third canto of "It Must Give Pleasure." The first of these, the theological fable of a "lasting visage in a lasting bush, / A face of stone in an unending red," recalls the "inexhaustible being" of the President and tells of a presence that moves unchangingly within the proliferating differences of history (CP, 400). It is the story of a *Heilsgeschichte*, of history as the movement of presence—a story Eliot tries to tell in *Murder*, but one he characterizes as servitude in the later *Four Quartets*. But the canto turns from this venerable tale—it "might have been"—to a new tale of origin, the Orphic tale of the origin "as it was." This is the story of detour and absence, of the "tremendous chords" of a poetry that can be sung only through the Orphic, or poetic, detour from poetry's literal subject, that is, by making metaphors or tropes of Eurydice in order to sustain (indirectly) her desired presence. Whereas the theological tale of the lasting visage is the story of the unchanging presence of presence, the poetical tale of the shepherd traces its perpetual absence. It remains, however, a story told in the rhetoric of metaphysics and representation, for the Orphic troping of poetry—its indirection and the provisional absence of its literal subject—is seen as merely a detour to or a sign of a trascendent presence it represents through the via negativa of poetic imagery.

Both the theological and the poetical stories of origin are, like the general's statue, monuments in the rhetoric of identity. But while the poetical displaces and supplements the theological, it is itself fissured by difference and seeming. The *as it was* of essential truth is marked by the *so they said* of the point of view or the tale, the ontological by the semiological. Like the Place du Puy, these monuments to the metaphysics of presence and absence finally trace the difference out of which they both emerge. The theological myth makes a difference to the poetical myth and vice versa—they are incommensurable, and Stevens suggests no ultimate validity for either of them—and both myths repeat this originating difference. Like the "early flowers . . . scattered" at the end of this canto, "Notes" proliferates tales of origin, and this multiplication insists upon a differentially conceived origin-in-difference.

Change, then, cannot be traced back to an essence out of which it emerges. Just as seeming is not something that happens to an original identity of being but rather marks being itself as the trace of semiological interference, so change appears in this second section

of "Notes" as repeated difference, as the eternal return of the interruption of the same by the latent opposite. This interference fractures the monumental generalization of identity into the "particulars of rapture." It is upon their interreference that "two things of
opposite natures seem to depend" and not upon the presence of
some immortal, inexhaustible essence; for Stevens, as for Nietzsche,
"The first leaf," the figure of an original, ideal identity transcending
difference, "is the tale / Of leaves."[8] The same depends upon the
trace of the other, the identical upon the different, unity upon the
couple or the plural; and thus "the partaker partakes of that which
changes him." He is constituted only within the differential and displacing relationships that characterize Stevens' invented world. The
differentiation that the originality of the plural or the "cold copulars" describes is, therefore, the "origin of change"—a change that,
unlike the continuous chronology of the President's metaphysics, is
irruptive and discontinuous, a change that always involves the displacement of and substitution for the one by the other it depends
on. Change for Stevens describes this endless dance of displacement
and substitution, a rapturous passion that redeploys the difference
of beginning by intervening in and subtly reinvigorating the "with-
ered scene" written in the single text of a chronological and metaphysical rhetoric.

Ozymandias' rejection of Nanzia Nunzio figures the nostalgic
dissatisfaction with the differences on which the things of the world
depend and with the "ancient cycle" of desire for a strictly naked
essence of identity. Nanzia Nunzio, whose name means "good mes-
senger or accredited ambassador," comes to Ozymandias as the
"contemplated spouse," the "woman stripped more nakedly / Than
nakedness," whose nudity would appear to reveal the identity of
truth unmediated by veiling ornaments.[9] She comes as truth itself,
as a constant identity within superficial differences. But as her name
implies, her revealing nakedness discloses her status as a sign of
something "beyond the burning body that I bear." That "burning,"
like the sun in the first canto of "Notes," thus presents itself as a
perplexing site of difference. Its arrival marks the refreshing return
of plurality and supplementation and reiterates the differential life

8. Clive (ed.), *The Philosophy of Nietzsche*, 507.
9. Glauco Cambon, *The Inclusive Flame: Studies in Modern American Poetry*
(Bloomington, 1965), 105.

of the sign and the semiological world. Nanzia Nunzio's assertion of identity—"I am the spouse"—is prefaced by the *as* that interrupts it with the mediations of rhetorical performance and seeming. Although she comes for Ozymandias as a "fictive covering," as a sign that again veils or disguises an endlessly desired but unobtainable truth, she simultaneously figures the fecund force of difference that quickens Stevens' world. Ozymandias throws the sign of difference away in a gesture similar to Eliot's dismissal of differential, historical time in *Murder in the Cathedral*. Nanzia Nunzio's speech, however, interferes with Ozymandias' interpretation and recalls Stevens' earlier advice to the ephebe, which insisted upon the differential character of signs as the essential and precious being of all things.

For Stevens, neither being nor seeming, neither the ontological phenomenon nor its semiological complement, can be individualized or abstracted from the interreferential relationship in which each emerges only as an interference with the other. Thus the unifying marriage of seeming to being, like the "mystic marriage" of sign to object in Eliot's dissertation, can never take place. Marriage in "Notes" is not a figure of classical representation, but must rather be distinguished as the essential relationship between signs. In "Description Without Place" that relationship occurs between the signifying column and the complementary sign of the dove. That relationship is not a marriage that collapses difference into unity, but an interference in which one sign displaces and substitutes for another. It is a differential and accidental balance—an example of the "balances [between signs] that happen / As a man and woman meet and love forthwith"—in which the "intrinsic couple" are only figuratively unified as one. The mystic marriage between the captain and Bawda in the fourth canto of "It Must Give Pleasure" is a similar reiteration of a differential balance between signs. Each "must the other take as sign, short sign / To stop the whirlwind, balk the elements" in a copular relationship that recalls the provisional "stop to watch / A definition growing certain" in the familiar *schwarmerei* of the semiological machine (CP, 386, 392, 401, 386). The marriage place is "neither heaven nor hell," but rather a semiological world in which signs find each other (as the captain found Bawda, a foundling like the supplemental MacCullough) in accidental balances or differential relationships that only provisionally stop the whirlwind of proliferating signs, the differentiating whirlwind being precisely the sustaining force repeated by the marriage itself. Whereas the metaphysical rhetoric of representation makes "of what we see . . . a place dependent on ourselves" and thereby seeks to reduce the copular balances of difference to a hierarchy of one-way dependence (of place on self, object on subject, outside on inside, seeming on being, or representation on presence), Stevens' marriages figure the irreducibly differential being of the semiological world, the marriage place characterized by the incidental or casual relationships among signs (CP, 401).[10]

Change thus occurs irruptively when one casually balanced system of signs substitutes for another similarly accidental arrangement, when one figure, interpretation, or text displaces another. This is change in the dynamic "Theatre / Of Trope"—in language and poetry—that interrupts the generalizing notions of chronology and being which interpret the differences between systems as insignificant and reducible to identity. But for Stevens, these balanced systems emerge differentially, and the metaphysical interpretation of difference as the sign of identity leads to "catalepsy," a disease of suspended animation that, if it is not displaced by another interpretation, withers and calcifies the life of language into the suspension of the representational statue (CP, 391). Like memory in Eliot's dissertation, change in Stevens redeploys the difference that interrupts the hallucinatory disease of identity. The ancient cycle of desire is the specific mechanism of this redeployment, for in the wish for truth are the irreducible characteristics constituting every sign system. Thus

There was a will to change, a necessitous
And present way, a presentation, a kind
Of volatile world, too constant to be denied. (CP, 397)

What is constant in Stevens' volatile world is the irruptive "will to change" that interferes in every systematic interpretation, every local balance of signs and words, with a "new relation" that "poetry constantly requires" for its differential life. As Stevens states in "Adagia," "The world is a force, not a presence," and in "Notes," "The freshness of transformation is / The freshness of a world" (OP, 178, 172; CP, 397–98). The changes traced in "Notes" do not follow the movement of a self-consistent essence, but rather describe the interruptions and displacements of identity in which all her-

10. Michel Benamou makes a similar observation in *L'Oeuvre—Monde de Wallace Stevens* (Lille, 1973), 329.

meneutical worlds begin. It is of "these beginnings, gay and green" that Stevens proposes the "suitable amours."

Stevens' invented world, then, is not describable in a classical rhetoric of representation. Rather, in this semiological world signs emerge in a copular relationship with each other, and all identities can be said to be products of this originating relationship. A sign, therefore, signifies neither presence nor absence—it does not represent something as such—but is rather the residue of this original and sustaining differentiating force. A sign is, as "Description Without Place" suggests, neither "The thing described, nor false facsimile," but an "artificial thing that exists," a process of seeming that makes a difference irreducible to the metaphysics of representation (CP, 344). "Notes" begins in such irreducible plurality and difference, for it begins at least twice—once with the epigram "To Henry Church" and again with the order to begin that opens Canto I. Such a multiple beginning redeploys the difference within which the invented world of "Notes" emerges.

The differential field of images, language, and signs Stevens outlines is not shadowed by a transcendent world of substance and essence for which terms like *presence* and *absence* have meaning. The copular other traced in the sign always turns out, like a Peircean object, to be another sign constituted in a differential relationship with the first. But this sign, on which the first seems to depend for its significance, is itself the trace of this differential relationship, the quick of the invention, and thus Stevens' semiological world describes a dynamic and complex field of proliferating differences. But this particular understanding of signs and language itself emerges only with a complementary point of view, with what Stevens calls the "human wish" for essential truth. This desire is similar to that both reflected and interrupted in *Murder in the Cathedral:* the wish for the closure of differences of historical interpretations upon a single, essential truth. In Eliot's play this desire led to a supplemental interpretation of Becket's death, and in Stevens it leads to the invention of supplementary figures of essence (the sun, the MacCullough, or the idea of man) and, therefore, to the writing of another name for the force of difference "that never could be named"—to the production of more tropes of identity that themselves redeploy the difference they are designed to close. The invented semiological world always begins with the supplementation of the name and the reiteration of the essential difference that is the "happy fecundity" celebrated in "Notes."

Thus there is in Stevens, as in Eliot, the irreducible interference of two incommensurable hermeneutical stances, two interpretations of signs and language—one characterized by the metaphysics of being and representation, and the other by the insistent difference that intervenes in the supplementary figures of the former. Just as, for Stevens, "Two things of opposite nature seem to depend / On one another," so poems themselves emerge within the differences these two points of view make to each other. Stevens' poetry suggests a semiological marriage place in which hermeneutical forces come face to face in a differential relationship that constitutes each as an interference with the other.

As the first canto of "It Must Give Pleasure" has it, within the "facile exercise" of representation (within, in other words, a hermeneutics that interprets signs and writing as the embodiment of an identifiable "bravest fundament" or a paternal "bleakest ancestor") the interference of the "difficultest rigor" can also be traced: "On the image of what we see, to catch from that / Irrational moment its unreasoning." Where the hermeneutics of representation produces images of original identity and presence, of the sun or the "heaven-haven" in which the signs of language can be seen as having a home, the "difficultest rigor" appears as a subversive gesture that reads in these supplemental things the traces of the difference that constitutes them. It intervenes in their ontological identity with the *as if* of seeming ("We are shaken by them as if they were"), and thus reinscribes in the image the difference to which representation's "later reason" is blind. The "difficultest rigor," then, is a style of reading the invented world of signs that works on the "image of what we see" and interferes with representation's images of identity by marking in their reasoning an incommensurable unreasoning. When the second canto's "blue woman looked and from her window named / The corals of the dogwood, cold and clear," her "coldly delineating," literal naming of the real was "clear and, except for the eye, without intrusion" (CP, 398, 400). In that exceptional intrusion—in the interfering difference delineation does not account for—Stevens catches the "unreasoning" of representation.

The blue woman's clear seeing is thus another story, like Eliot's in *Murder in the Cathedral,* of the end of difference in the closure of signs upon an essential identity of meaning. The Canon Aspirin performs a similar rhetorical declamation about the "sensible ecstasy" of his sister who, by hiding her daughters under the "rigid statement" of "simple names," earns the Canon's approval by apparently "rejecting dreams" and fighting off the "barest phrases"—by, that is, rejecting the intrusions of language that would keep her from seeing her daughters' identities "as they were." But this story of clear seeing, of an observer-elect, is interfered with by the frame tale of the Canon, which marks the story of clairvoyance as a declaimed rhetorical performance. Only within this textual frame, within a language that is performative and not representational, can the story of ontological being be told. Thus the Canon's "fugue / Of praise" begins by outlining the metaphysics of representation, by sketching a figure in which being and seeming can be rigorously separated and individualized so that they have no bearing on each other, but it modulates rapidly into something else. This figure is displaced by that of the "whole, / The complicate, the amassing harmony" in which there is never "a choice / Between excluding things," because each thing bears within itself the trace of the other—they are "things / That in each other are included." The complicate folds back on itself in the same way that the clairvoyance declaimed in the Canon's poem (a figure of the closure of seeming in being, differences in identity) doubles as a scene performed in the semiological theater of trope. The choice can never be between one thing or another, between one independent hermeneutical stance or another, since "it was not a choice / Between, but of" (CP, 402, 403). Because both being and seeming, identity and difference, are constituted differentially and are included in each other, the logic of either/or choice ceases to be meaningful.

The figure of the complicate itself must not be conceived as escaping this perplexity or as being the name of an individualized and determinate truth, for it emerges here as another name "for something that never could be named," as another redeployment of the difference its image calcifies into the presence of a delineated identity. The name obscures difference by imposing individuality. Canto VII of "It Must Give Pleasure" recognizes that "to impose is not / To discover" and expresses the human wish for an unimposed, unmediated truth.

> It is possible, possible, possible. It must
> Be possible. It must be that in time
> The real will from its crude compoundings come,

Seeming, at first, a beast disgorged, unlike,
Warmed by a desperate will. (CP, 404)

But this possibility itself maintains the "fiction of an absolute" that
marks the disgorged *real* with the "crude compoundings" of difference, with the *as if* that doubles discovery with willed imposition
and the intrusions of "later reason." We need only recall the blue
woman, the metaphysical President, and the sigil-like ephebe of the
fifth canto of "It Must Be Abstract" to point out the imposition of
the absolute repeated by naming's "bitter utterance." And yet, like
the Canon who had to choose, the ephebe is called upon to name
again, for it is by the imposition and supplementation of this name
that difference is redeployed and writing begins. The name in Stevens is always interrupted by the *as if* that perplexes the absolute it
names, and in this way difference intervenes in the named identity.
At the same time, however, the name conceals difference in the "fiction of an absolute" or in the "inexhaustible being" the name inevitably suggests. This effacement of difference produces, as "Bouquet
of Roses in Sunlight" states, the *real* that seems "So far beyond the
rhetorician's touch," the discovered identity nevertheless indelibly
marked by the imposed seeming of rhetoric (CP, 384, 431). Writing complicates the figure of the absolute with the interference of
difference, and the figure of difference with that of the absolute, in
an energetic circulation, a semiological whirlwind of complicated
interreferentiality. At the center of this spinning world of words is
not the reconciling nucleus of truth, but a differentiating space of
dead air.

For Stevens, the pleasure of this "merely circulating" affects the
human, nostalgic desire for the closure of the differential world of
words upon a monumental center of essence or truth. The invented
world of language is always the site of the "Whistle . . . for the
mate," the nostalgic call to an essence beyond words' rhetorical
horizon (CP, 149, 405). This call is endlessly repeated and is the
force behind the supplemental figures constructed to fulfill its unending desire. These supplements, by recalling the casual artifice of
their imposition, repeat the whistle and begin again the ancient
cycle of desire. This circulation traces the differentiation that opens
and sustains the invented world of words, a constituting difference
only nominally obscured (because simultaneously redeployed) by
each monumental supplement, each link in an unending chain of

differential substitutions. Stevens' final advice to the ephebe is to "whistle and bugle" (to repeat words' unavoidable call for the mate) but to stop just short: "stop in your preludes, practicing / Mere repetitions." The ephebe is advised to write, in other words, the marginal notes, or "preludes," that defer the central book or musical composition to which they implicitly refer, and thus to repeatedly redeploy the difference on which all writing depends. It is the exercise of this force and the tracing of difference in the monumentally identical that is, for Stevens, the way "we enjoy like men" the endlessly circulating way of writing:

> . . . the way a leaf
> Above the table spins its constant spin,
> So that we look at it with pleasure, look
>
> At it spinning its eccentric measure. (CP, 406)

This is the eccentric, energetic spin of the differential whirlwind of language, the source of the poet's pleasure and the life of his "fluent mundo." Always there is the metaphysics of representation and the name, the "unprovoked sensation" to close the differential play of signs, to "name . . . flatly, waste no words / Check [the fluent world's] evasions, hold you to yourself." This is the straight talk of the "Sorbonne," the rhetoric that predicts the day when the irrational is rational, when the *as if* of difference will finally be reduced to the *is* of identity. But always within this discourse Stevens traces the interference of the "moving contour," the aberration or distortion that is "a change not quite completed," the exception that keeps the world of words from speaking truth "straight" and keeps it revolving in its differential spin.[11] Always there is the remainder, the indelible trace of difference,

> The accent of deviation in the living thing
> That is its life preserved, the effort to be born
> Surviving being born, the event of life. (OP, 96)

In this *clinamen* differential life is preserved. The spinning world of "Notes" closes only as it began, with contrived, supplemental artifice. The excessive remaining canto refigures a "war that never ends" and a copular, differential

11. Joseph Riddel has noted how the final image of "Notes" repeats the differential pleasure of the poem in "Interpreting Stevens: An Essay on Poetry and Thinking," *boundary 2*, I (Fall, 1972), 91.

. . . plural, a right and left, a pair,
Two parallels that meet if only in
The meeting of their shadows or that meet
In a book in a barrack, a letter from Malay. (CP, 407)

Here is no final collapse of two into one, but the reinscription of "shadows" and writing; here are the "petty syllabi" of the poet that, by "inevitably modulating," trace again the irreducibly differential life of Stevens' invented world.

Three
Parasites and Burglars

In Eliot's dissertation, meaning appeared as a site of ideal significance always interfered with—productively, as it turned out—by
the endless differentiations of memory. In Stevens' "Notes," meaning was described as the problem of the sweeping generalizations we
add to language that obscure the subtle differentiations upon which
language and thought depend. But the concluding talk in Eliot's series of lectures given at Harvard during the winter of 1932–1933
presents us with an even more extraordinary image of poetic meaning. Toward the end of his talk, Eliot stated: "The chief use of the
'meaning' of a poem, in the ordinary sense, may be (for here again I
am speaking of some kinds of poetry and not all) to satisfy one
habit of the reader, to keep his mind diverted and quiet, while the
poem does its work upon him: much as the imaginary burglar is
always provided with a bit of nice meat for the house-dog. This is a
normal situation of which I approve" (UPUC, 151). The image does
not make clear the precise nature of poetic work other than to define it as a particular type of theft, but it does underscore a certain
subreption that allows this theft to take place. According to this
image, poetry works only through the mediation of a clever diversion or detour, a rerouting of the reader's attention away from
the theft that the poem is actually accomplishing and toward a gift,
the "meat" of the poem, that it freely gives the reader. This meaty

gift is meaningful to poetry only because it obscures poetry's transgressive theft. Here, meaning subreptitiously protects the transgression that is poetry's true work by hiding it in an illusion through which it appears to be a presentation or gift rather than a thievish crime. The subreptitious relationship between meaning and the poem thus dramatizes what Eliot calls the "normal situation" of poetry.

Eliot writes throughout his criticism about meaning, often in an effort to describe the relationship between the meaning of poetry and the music of poetry. His emphasis upon the originary role of music in poetry—in one essay he notes that a poem "may tend to realize itself first as a particular rhythm before it reaches its expression in words, and . . . this rhythm may bring to birth the idea and the image" (OPP, 32)—recalls a similar emphasis upon music developed by Nietzsche in *The Birth of Tragedy from the Spirit of Music*. Nietzsche's elaboration upon the interlocutive relationship between Dionysus and Apollo profoundly informs Eliot's criticism, particularly when that criticism explores the place of meaning in poetry and music. In *The Birth of Tragedy,* Apollo appears as the figurative "god of all plastic powers and the soothsaying god." The lucent "god of light," reason, and truth, Apollo embodies the *principium individuationis,* and thus stands as the god of spatial resolution. His realm is that of the plastic, spatial arts, and his mastery of space renders him the "god of individuation and just boundaries." Apollo draws boundary lines, and by so doing he reconciles spatial differences into a unified pattern; under his jurisdiction, everything falls into place. By thus enforcing limits and boundaries, Apollo allows for the individuation in which things are only themselves and protects the integrity of the individual from duplicity and disarray. Nietzsche asserts that through the clarifying lucidity afforded by the god of light, the Hellenic cosmos is resolved into a figure of organized space in which the either/or logic of Aristotelian categorization functions without interference. Apollo is the god of the proper, of propriety, and of property—of that which reflects the security of ownership and of one's own place.[1]

But this secure resolution, with its proper, spatial boundaries, is for Nietzsche only an illusionary and protective compensation for

1. Friedrich Nietzsche, *"The Birth of Tragedy" and "The Genealogy of Morals,"* trans. Francis Golffing (New York, 1956), 21, 22, 65.

the Greeks' earlier, horrifying look into "the abyss" of nature. He draws his image from the sun: "After an energetic attempt to focus on the sun, we have, by way of remedy almost, dark spots before our eyes when we turn away. Conversely, the luminous images of the Sophoclean heroes—those Apollonian masks—are the necessary productions of a deep look into the horror of nature; luminous spots, as it were, designed to cure an eye hurt by the ghastly night." Apollo, and the spatial propriety he stands for, thus appear as a fictive light, a hallucinatory radiance that mediates (and thereby protects the Greeks from) the truly blinding light of abysmal nature. Where lucidity and propriety appear—where Apollo, the lucent one, presents himself—there, for Nietzsche, is the diversionary and protective illusion; there insight and truths arise only as "the luminous afterimage which kind nature provides our eyes after a look into the abyss." [2]

In fierce opposition to the spatializing figure of Apollo stands Dionysus, who for Nietzsche represents the creative tendency toward the "nonvisual art of music." Whereas Apollo embodies the desire for the propriety of just boundaries, Dionysus, Nietzsche's image of the "ecstatic artist," refuses the confines of boundaries and thereby interferes with the illusion of propriety: "Lest the Apollonian tendency freeze all form into Egyptian rigidity, and in attempting to prescribe its orbit to each particular wave inhibit the movement of the lake, the Dionysiac flood tide periodically destroys all the little circles in which the Apollonian will would confine Hellenism." Like the "difficultest rigor" with which Stevens breaks into the cataleptic order of reason and logic, Dionysiac music—the temporal, processional, creative tendency—inhabits, like a parasite, the rigid spatial pattern of Apollo's domain and transgresses its boundaries, thereby disclosing its inadequacy and robbing it of its absolute truth. For Nietzsche, music alone "allows us to understand the delight felt at the annihilation of the individual," at the ecstatic demolition of the precise and lucid clarity that results from the imposed Apollonian law of *principium individuationis*. In this principle "the eternal goal of the original Oneness, namely its redemption through illusion, accomplishes itself," but this unity, the "ground of Being," is itself an energetic site of difference. "Eversuffering and contradictory," it "time and again has need of rapt vision and delightful illusion" to redeem and resolve itself. These rapt visions, however, are

2. *Ibid.*, 59–60, 61.

never other than the repetitious, practical illusions of Apollo, each of which emerges only as another point of Dionysiac interference.[3]

Thus for Nietzsche, Dionysiac music repeatedly breaks into the bounds of propriety established by the illusionary Apollonian patterning of space. This perpetual interference cannot be excluded from the images of Apollonian language. Rather, it inhabits it like a parasite that is nevertheless the "innermost core" of language. Music "resists any adequate treatment by language, for the simple reason that music, in referring to primordial contradiction and pain, symbolizes a sphere which is both earlier than appearance and beyond it. Once we set it over against music, all appearance becomes mere analogy. So it happens that language, the organ and symbol of appearance, can never succeed in bringing the innermost core of music to the surface." Apollonian imagery—language—creates the hallucination of appearance, of independent individuals dwelling in their own proper sites and distinguished from other individuals by "just boundaries." No interferences, no boundary disputes, disturb the peace of this illusion, and in this way Apollo appears to resolve the original contradiction of "Being" by obscuring the difference that constitutes it. It is within this illusion that truth as noncontradictory identity first emerges, but its appearance is for Nietzsche always interfered with by the original contradiction of Dionysiac music. Thus Nietzsche's emphasis is upon the interference of the noise that disturbs Apollo's harmonizing illusions. Musical dissonance is a polyphony of differences, a noise irreducible to univocality, a site of difference in which multiple tones intrude on each other in a constant clash that transgresses the orderly laws of harmony. Dionysiac music is the incarnation of this essential heterogeneity and difference.[4]

Apollo interprets and resolves the dissonance of Dionysus, which appears only in the transgression of Apollo's illusory boundaries. Thus the Greek drama presents the "coming and going of the shuttle as it weaves the tissue."

> In the final effect of tragedy the Dionysiac element triumphs once again: its closing sounds are such as were never heard in the Apollonian realm. The Apollonian illusion reveals its identity as the veil thrown over the Dionysiac meanings for the duration of the play, and yet the illusion is so potent that at its close the Apollonian drama is projected into a sphere

3. *Ibid.*, 19, 24, 65, 101, 32.
4. *Ibid.*, 46, 145.

where it begins to speak with Dionysiac wisdom, thereby denying itself and its Apollonian concreteness. The difficult relations between the two elements in tragedy may be symbolized by a fraternal union between the two deities: Dionysos speaks the language of Apollo, but Apollo, finally, the language of Dionysos.

Since neither god has a language of his own, the forward propulsion of Greek drama derives from the mutually parasitic relationship in which each god feeds off of and steals away the other's language, repeating it as his own in a continual transgression that deploys time and again the contradictory dissonance Nietzsche names "Being." The repeated engaging of this relationship "reminds us that conditions are aspects of one and the same Dionysiac phenomenon, of that spirit which playfully shatters and rebuilds the teeming world of individuals—much as, in Heracleitus, the plastic power of the universe is compared to a child tossing pebbles or building a sand pile and then destroying what he has built." [5]

Nietzsche's discussion of Apollo and Dionysus throws light upon Eliot's burglary image and its disclosure of the relationship between meaning and poetic work. Just as Apollo and Dionysus emerge in a mutually parasitic relationship, so the meaning of a poem—the meat, substance, truth, or subject sought by the reader—appears along with the poem's actual work as a calming diversion that allows the burglary to take place. Such meaning can be seen as the poem's meaty core of significance that the reader ingests or devours, but since that meat is a subreption of the work the poem actually does, the reader eats a meal only of airy illusion. Not a host in which transcendent sustenance is incarnated, meaning rather emerges as an Apollonian staging of divinely significant food, as a trick that throws the reader off the poem's scent and hides from view the burglary that is always in progress whenever the meaty meaning appears. And what is burglary but a transgression of boundaries, a breaking into, opening up, and stealing away of property? In Eliot's image, however, such transgression of the proper is not an aberration of bad poetry, not an occasional criminality that befalls poetry from some depraved outside, but it is rather the approved and normal work that the poem does. Like the musical dissonance that is for Nietzsche the incarnation of contradictory self-difference, and therefore the interference that breaks into every Apollonian illusion

5. Ibid., 131, 143–44.

of just boundaries, the work of the poem is a perpetual burglary, a raid on property and a transgression of the boundaries that would hold the proper to itself. Poetic meaning masks the poem's law-breaking work.

When Eliot writes directly about music, however, he often attempts to affirm music and rhythm as the privileged expressions of truth and meaning and to exclude from them the parasitic interferences of difference and error. This exclusion recalls similar Eliotic strategies in *Murder* and in the dissertation, but it is an Apollonian gesture that, nevertheless, is finally interrupted by a Dionysiac duplicity. Words and names, the symbols of language, can take us only so far toward the significant fringe of feeling that "music can express." Harry Antrim notes that, for Eliot, "language may inherently possess structures which in their rhythm and music bear correspondence to the ground of human emotion," an observation consistent with Eliot's privileging of music and rhythm, in which he points out that a particular rhythm may reflect the origin or ground of a poem, giving "birth to the idea and the image" (OPP, 93, 32).[6] Where language fails—where it is fundamentally mediated by the limitations of the nameable—music succeeds, transcending those limitations and taking us back to poetry's source. This, for Eliot, is the role of the "auditory imagination," a faculty that, through musical rhythm, provides access to the purity of a grounding site. "What I call the 'auditory imagination' is the feeling for syllable and rhythm, penetrating far below the conscious levels of thought and feeling, invigorating every word; sinking to the most primitive and forgotten, returning to the origin and bringing something back, seeking the beginning and the end" (UPUC, 119).

For Eliot, music is able to move beyond the limited nature of words that forever renders them incapable of expressing the origin. Rhythm invigorates words by reaching beyond them toward an "unattainable timelessness," a "stillness of painting or sculpture" that appears as the unnameable fringe beyond the pale of words and from which words nevertheless draw sustenance. It is toward this original stillness that Eliot writes his poetry, which he desires to be "so transparent that in reading it we are intent on what the poem *points at,* and not on the poetry itself." Through such poetry, Eliot

6. Harry T. Antrim, *T. S. Eliot's Concept of Language: A Study of its Development* (Gainesville, 1971), 45–46.

seeks to "get *beyond poetry,* as Beethoven, in his later works, strove to get *beyond music.*"[7]

Although music is the invigorating life of the word, and although it expresses the "border of . . . feelings" that lie beyond poetry's words, music is at the same time poetry's death. "We can never emulate music, because to arrive at the condition of music would be the annihilation of poetry." Eliot states that the problem with Milton, for example, is that his poetry is too musical: "The emphasis is on the sound, not the vision, upon the word, not the idea." The result is a labyrinthine maze of sound or rhetorical noise in which one wanders without a visionary map, without the Ariadne's thread of an idea to follow to the maze's significant outside. For Eliot, the job of meaning is to check this abysmal maze of sound, to arrange its dissonant noise into the harmonized uniformity of an idea. Thus Milton should have learned that "the music of verse is strongest in poetry which has a definite meaning expressed in the properest words" (OPP, 93, 179, 183).

Between music and meaning in poetry, then, Eliot posits a mutually parasitic relationship similar to the one Nietzsche outlines between Dionysus and Apollo in Greek drama. To be itself at all, to stand out from the dangerous noise of its origin, poetry must speak with a language other than music, a language of vision, idea, and intellectual meaning that "supplements the music by another means." This supplementary language adds to poetry's musical maze the harmonizing meaning that lifts the poem out of the noisy "condition of music" and steals away its sound toward vision, its rhythm toward idea, in a move that distances and protects the poem from the dangers of its origin: "The meaning of the poem may be . . . something remote from its origins." Like the Apollonian subreption of Dionysus, meaning establishes boundaries of sense within the originating rhythms of poetry. But, as Eliot often asserts, "the music of poetry is not something which exists apart from the meaning," and thus it emerges in a constituting and irreducibly differential relationship without which there would be neither music nor meaning (OPP, 179; SW, 146; OPP, 22, 21). Music invigorates the words of poetry that translate its dissonant noise into univocal

7. T. S. Eliot, "The Art of Poetry," introduction to Paul Valéry, *Collected Works of Paul Valéry* (15 vols.; New York, 1958), VII, p. xiv; William Harmon, "T. S. Eliot's Raids on the Inarticulate," *Publications of the Modern Language Association,* XCI (May, 1976), 459 (n. 22).

meaning, but that dangerous noise continues to inhabit the meaning that both excludes it and cannot exist without it.

Such a translation repeats Apollo's interpretation of the abyss of original contradiction figured by Dionysus, the spatializing of musical dissonance into the resolved pattern of the image. In Nietzsche, this reconciling pattern is only a provisional and protective illusion, a figurative lucidity or "luminous afterimage," that obscures the contradiction, dissonance, and difference that constitutes it; in Eliot, this pattern is often affirmed as the reconciling identity of absolute truth, or as the single, eternal still point and center of the turning world of time. For Eliot, the problem with *Hamlet* is that it has no such central lucidity, no punctual site of truth, no meaningfully coherent "objective equivalent" to pattern and resolve Hamlet's strange actions. The feeling of the play is "very difficult to localize," because what lies at the center of *Hamlet* is darkness, not light. "The subject might conceivably have expanded into a tragedy like [*Othello* or *Coriolanus*], intelligible, self-complete, in the sunlight. *Hamlet*, like the sonnets, is full of some stuff that the writer could not drag to light." *Hamlet* is contradictory, full of interferences and noise that resist harmonization into a univocal aspect like, for example, the "suspicion of Othello, the infatuation of Antony, or the pride of Coriolanus" (SW, 100).

Hamlet, according to Eliot, fails exactly where the plays of John Marston succeed. Whereas Hamlet's excessive actions do not bespeak the lucidity of any single motivation or meaning, Marston's plays always give us "the sense of something behind, more real than any of his personages and their action," and it is for this reason that Marston "establishes himself among the writers of genius." This "underlying serenity" reconciles the "tumultuousness of the action, and the ferocity and horror of certain parts of the play," into a meaningful pattern behind the pattern "into which the characters deliberately involve themselves." Unlike in Shakespeare's perplexing play, in Marston's plays there is no noise that cannot be interpreted as meaningful, no interrupting parasites at the feast of meaning the reader enjoys. Eliot equates this higher reality of the underpattern to the "Fate" of the ancient world, to the "delicate theology" of Christianity, and to the "crudities of psychological or economic necessity" characteristic of the modern world (EE, 190, 194). In each temporal epoch, the underpattern suggests a reconciling identity, an imminent still point that organizes the differences of time into a meaningful uniformity. Similarly, in Marston's plays the under-pattern is the self-consistent core or idea represented by the play's differing actions.

The essay on Marston, while deploying the figure of the under-pattern, nevertheless interferes with it in a way that recalls Nietzsche's critique of Apollonian truth. Eliot suggests that the underpattern is a problematic dark spot, a luminous afterimage similar to the illusionary truths of Apollo. In a brief qualification, he describes the underpattern as "the kind of pattern which we perceive in our own lives only at rare moments of inattention and detachment, drowsing in sunlight" (EE, 194). This higher reality cannot be thought of only as a unified core, for it emerges as constituted by a deployment of difference, mediation, and interference. Only by turning away from and forgetting the interference without which it never appears can the pattern be read as the sign of reconciliation, of self-complete, noncontradictory meaning. The moment of this lucid insight is at the same time a moment of protective blindness, a moment of illusion and of storytelling. This is particularly apparent in *Murder in the Cathedral*, in which Becket counsels the chorus that their sufferings will be turned to "sudden painful joy / When the figure of God's purpose is made complete," when, that is, the meaningful underpattern of the eternal resolves the contradictory mazes of time and history. Then,

> You shall forget these things, toiling in the household,
> You shall remember them, drowsing by the fire,
> When age and forgetfulness sweeten memory
> Only like a dream that has often been told
> And often been changed in the telling. (CPP, 208–209)

These mediations disclose the purely practical significance of the "figure of God's purpose" and mark it as a "luminous afterimage which kind nature provides our eyes after a look into the abyss." [8] Becket's final line echoes the diversionary property of the Apollonian and Eliotic illusion of pattern, propriety, and meaning: "Human kind cannot bear very much reality" (CPP, 209).

Like Apollo finally speaking with the language of Dionysus, meaning—which is both real and illusionary, both meaty substance and mere sleight-of-hand trickery—ultimately repeats the contra-

8. Nietzsche, *Birth of Tragedy*, 61.

dictory noise it appears to organize into a harmonic pattern. Meaning in Eliot is a site of insistent difference always inhabited by an internal contradiction, by an unwanted but unexcludable parasite that steals away meaning's most valuable property—its self-consistency. Meaning, then, is the trace or evidence of a burglary, of a constituting interference or transgression that is nothing less than the theft of the proper itself, for meaning can be thought only along with the difference or noise that robs it of its propriety. The "normal situation" of poetry, like the normal project of Greek drama, is its repetition of this essential burglary, of the resolving of difference in a diverting meaning that ultimately recalls the trick of its composition and the contradiction of its origin.

Just as in Stevens there is never a language so self-consistent that its meaning is not interrupted by unfilterable interferences, so in Eliot meaning is repeatedly constituted as this very interference of message and noise. Although much of Eliot's writing privileges certain metaphors of self-consistent literal meaning (like the "still point" and the "underpattern"), it repeatedly interferes with these figures by disclosing in them the contradictory difference—most often, the irreducible possibility that they are a practical trick of rhetoric and not the signs of an absolute, essential truth—that is their initial and constituting condition. This interference is the *modus operandi* of Eliot's and Stevens' poetry, for both poetries insist upon this constituting difference that keeps words from falling into place in a determining hermeneutical scheme. In Stevens, words spin in an "eccentric measure" never completely controlled by an ordering intention or law; in Eliot, words redeploy the noise that inhabits all harmonious patterns of meaning.

But words also spin eccentrically in Eliot, and their wayward motion can be traced in his first drawing-room drama, *The Family Reunion*. The metaphors of the title suggest the controllable circling of family members around a home, the site at which their different journeys and lives can be recovered in a moment of reunion. This desire for the collapsing of differences at a punctual site of reunification permeates the major critical approaches to the play. Interpreting it as a religious and mythical drama that traces Harry's spiritual election, or as a sacramental drama that reconciles the differences between past and present, or as a psychological drama of the reintegration of Harry's psyche, such criticism repeats the closed circle of sin and expiation, of fall and redemption, of dispersal and recollection, outlined by the play's title.

The waywardness of *The Family Reunion*'s language, however, interferes with the apparently privileged metaphors of its title. What is reflected by this waywardness is not the closure of a hermeneutical circle, but rather a certain prodigality, a constituting difference inhabiting the language, that ultimately breaks into the closed circle traced by that title. The "family reunion" and the closure it implies are continually interrupted by a perplexing problem. In this play the topical site is inhabited by a parasite—the *topos* by the *tropos,* identity by difference—that cannot finally be excluded, and it is in the redeployment of this problematic interference that Eliot's drama steals away the propriety of the hermeneutical figures of circularity and closure alluded to by its title.

The Family Reunion is oriented around Wishwood, the ancestral home and referential center of the family Monchensey. As Agatha points out, it is the place Harry desired during his wanderings in the tropics.

> Harry must often have remembered Wishwood—
> The nursery tea, the school holiday,
> The daring feats on the old pony,
> And thought to creep back through the little door— (CPP, 228)

It is also, however, the potential site of a forgetfulness that seeks to overlook the events of the past few years and thus to annul time and the differences it has engendered. Amy hopes that when Harry returns home, "He will wish to forget" the intervening years of his wanderings and particularly the death of his wife (CPP, 229). Her desire is thus to close the interval of time and the familial dispersal it has precipitated by simply obliterating all temporal differences. As she tells Agatha,

> Nothing is changed, Agatha, at Wishwood.
> Everything is kept as it was when he left it,
> Except the old pony, and the mongrel setter
> Which I had to have destroyed.
> Nothing has been changed. I have seen to that. (CPP, 228)

In a 1938 letter to E. Martin Browne, Eliot explains, "The tragedy [of *The Family Reunion*] is the tragedy of Amy, of a person living on

Will alone."[9] This will is, in effect, a will to reunify, to close the family circle upon its original site, and thus to gather together temporal and spatial differences. The retrieval of the family from its dispersal requires the maintenance of its topological center, the site at which this reunification can occur. It is for this that Amy has lived.

> . . . I keep Wishwood alive
> To keep the family alive, to keep them together,
> To keep me alive, and I live to keep them. (CPP, 227)

For Amy, the House of Monchensey lives only while its topological center remains fixed in the house itself, and it is this reference point, and the Dowager who resides there, that provisionally orient and organize the temporal and spatial dispersal of fathers and sons, mothers and daughters, brothers and sisters, into the genealogical order of a house. Harry points to Amy as the family's center of reference when he observes that "Everything has always been referred back to mother" (CPP, 258). Amy's desire thus represents a will to overpower difference, a will to achieve the closure of the family circle achieved by the maintenance of its fixed and central place, its *topos* of reference.

But all is not secure in this center. The very name of the house, Wishwood, suggests that it is the site of longing, and the play opens with a prayer to the punctual center of all topologies, the sun, which presents itself at Wishwood only in the figure of its eclipse.

> O Sun, that was once so warm, O Light that was taken
>   for granted
> When I was young and strong, and sun and light unsought for
> And the night unfeared and the day expected
> And the clocks could be trusted, tomorrow assured
> And time would not stop in the dark. (CPP, 225)

No longer illuminated by a sun whose light and warmth can be unquestioningly relied upon, the house has fallen into disrepair. Charles, for example, tells Harry that the "cellar could do with a little attention," and Ivy observes that old Hawkins has "let the rock garden go to rack and ruin, / And he's nearly half blind." A similar decay has taken place in Amy herself, for Warburton notes that "the whole machine is weak / And running down" (CPP, 233, 261).

9. E. Martin Browne, *The Making of T. S. Eliot's Plays* (Cambridge, 1969), 107.

What is at stake in the figure of Wishwood is not simply the dilapidation of a country house in the north of England, but also the circular pattern of issuance and return traced by the play's titular metaphor, the family reunion—the metaphor of the collapse of difference into unity. Wishwood stands at the center of the family as its *topos* of origin, but its space is distinctly textual, for Wishwood is the textual record of the history and lineage of the House of Monchensey.

> And what is spoken remains in the room, waiting for the
>   future to hear it
> . . . .
> The agony in the curtained bedroom, whether of birth
>   or of dying,
> Gathers in to itself all the voices of the past, and
>   projects them into the future.
> . . . .
> The whisper, the transparent deception
> The keeping up of appearances
> The making the best of a bad job
> All twined and tangled together, all are recorded. (CPP, 270–71)

The play's setting is thus a trope of a book, and its action takes place within a textual topology—a figure upon which the entire play meditates.

The book as house and the house as book—like much in *The Family Reunion,* this equation recalls Henry James. The name *Warburton* and Agatha's reference to the "very *jolly* corner" echo the novelist's texts, and the equation above brings to mind his preface to *The Portrait of a Lady.* There James describes himself as a builder who "should clearly have to pile brick upon brick for the creation of an interest" and who "would build large—in fine embossed vaults and pointed arches, as who should say, and yet never let it appear that the chequered pavement, the ground under the reader's feet, fails to stretch at every point to the base of the walls." What he builds is the "house of fiction," the structure pierced by "a number of possible windows not to be reckoned" and that is "as nothing without the posted presence of the watcher—without, in other words, the consciousness of the artist." [10] The fictional house is the site of this consciousness, and in it the author appears as the head of the house-

10. Henry James, *The Art of the Novel* (New York, 1934), 52, 46.

hold, the father of the family, and the observer-elect who reconciles the many different windows, or points of view. Wishwood, however, is this Jamesian metaphor gone bad, for it reflects a book in which such an authoritative consciousness is either unstable or missing, a house that, like Canterbury Cathedral and the "castle-fortress-home" in Stevens' "Notes," awaits its restoration in the return of its head. Harry is referred to as "the head" and "consciousness" of a family that impatiently awaits his return, expecting him then to take command at Wishwood and restore to order a physical structure ravaged by time and a genealogical line frayed by difference and dispersal (CPP, 229, 254, 275, 261). Such a return would restore to both House and book a proper head or reconciling consciousness, a topic or central *topos* of reference. Awaiting Harry's return, Wishwood marks itself as the topic-less text of desire. In Stevens, "not to have is the beginning of desire" (CP, 382), and it is with the redeployment of this ancient cycle that *The Family Reunion* begins.

The topology of the play outlines the North as the site of a broken familial and textual circle that expects to close upon the certainty of a fixed center. It is thus the site of a sacramental hermeneutics similar to that which intervenes in *Murder in the Cathedral*. The South, on the other hand, marks the perpetual deferral of any such closure. As Maud Bodkin points out, the South has been the scene against which Harry "has spent the years of his young strength wandering idle and tormented from one luxury hotel to another." [11] It is the place of the borrowed home, where the waywardness of the family never leads back to a proper home but only to the hotels that are perpetual displacements of a home. The South is thus marked by a constant turning or wandering, a troping that underlines this area's tropological nature. Agatha notes that Harry has been "Wandering in the tropics / Or against the painted scene of the Mediterranean." Unlike the book of Wishwood, which seems to circle around a central *topos* of significance, the circularity of the South is a circulation without closure. There is no *topos* proper to the books of the South, for the "circulating libraries" found there have by definition no proper home. However, it is only within this tropical space, in the perpetual circulation of wandering books, wayward family members, and homeless tropes, that the sun ever appears. "I would go south in the winter," says Ivy. "I would follow

11. Maud Bodkin, *The Quest for Salvation in an Ancient and a Modern Play* (London, 1941), 40.

the sun" (CPP, 228, 225). Like the sun in Stevens' "Description Without Place," the sun in *The Family Reunion* shines only along with the eclipsing interference that marks it as not simply the punctual *topos* of lucidity and truth, but also as a painted scene in a theater of trope. And thus like the Greek drama described by Nietzsche, Eliot's play deploys a perplexingly multiple space that is at once topological and tropological.

Like a book in the circulating libraries, Harry wanders in the tropics.

> . . . no direction
> Leads anywhere but round and round in that vapour—
> Without purpose, and without principle of conduct. (CPP, 235)

No law organizes this wandering into a closure, for the tropics articulate a declination from any purpose or principle of conduct. The house Harry describes himself as differs significantly from the decaying structure of Wishwood: "I am the old house / With the noxious smell and the sorrow before morning," the house permeated by the "noxious smell untraceable in the drains / Inaccessible to the plumbers" and the "unspoken voice of sorrow in the ancient bedroom / At three o'clock in the morning." Unlike Wishwood, this house does not await the return of a topic, for it is a place not of the "posted presence of the watcher" but of the unspeakable and the uncanny, a place of interferences and untraceable noises and smells, a place constituted by unresolvable difference. Such a house is a scandal at Wishwood, a scandal to the hermeneutics that envisions a unified topic at the center of the book, for like the tropological space of the South and the noisy mazes of sound in Milton, it suggests a labyrinth in which every corridor leads only "to another / Or to a blank wall" (CPP, 234, 252).

But there is a certain wandering in the House of Monchensey as well, for the genealogy of the family does not follow the economy of an unbranching line that would properly account for the family members by tracing their origins back to a single, paternal root. Rather, the history of the House of Monchensey is a history of displacements, of a fraying of the family line repeated by the metaphoric death of the father and the subsequent substitution of a plurality of different women (Amy and her sisters) into the empty place of authority. Agatha observes of Harry's father:

> He hid his strength beneath unusual weakness,
> The diffidence of a solitary man:

Where he was weak he recognised your mother's power,
And yielded to it. (CPP, 273)

The result is the displacement or beheading by Amy of this familial head.

There were many years
Before she succeeded in making terms with Wishwood,
Until she took your father's place, and reached the
        point where
Wishwood supported her, and she supported Wishwood. (CPP, 274)

Amy rushes in to supplement the vacancy at the head of the family, a
vacancy guarded by Harry's similarly "triumphant aunts."

We never heard him mentioned, but in some way or another
We felt that he was always here.
But when we would have grasped for him, there was only
        a vacuum
Surrounded by whispering aunts. (CPP, 260)

The history of the House of Monchensey traces the interruptions in
the lineage of authority and deploys the position of familial head
not as a site of reconciliation and unity, but as a vacuous *topos* of
difference. The father is missing—the "posted presence" or univocal "principle of conduct" fails to appear—and in his place
emerges a polyphony of female voices and a multiplicity of collateral
relations.

Thus the prodigality of the tropical South, the place of the eccentric circulation of metaphor, also appears in the North, in the supposedly closed topology of the family circle and the topical book.
The topical wanders; it is inhabited by the tropical and emerges as a
site of difference that the play's characters hope Harry's return will
solve. Such a solution, akin to Eliot's project to close the differences
of history in the unifying solution of *Murder*'s sacramental perspective, is often attempted in *The Family Reunion*, where it consistently
appears as a type of murder. This violence is nowhere more apparent than in the family's response to Harry's unnamed wife. Amy as-
sociates her with the excesses of the tropics.

She never wanted
Harry's relations or Harry's old friends;
She never wanted to fit herself to Harry,
But only to bring Harry down to her own level.

A restless shivering painted shadow
In life, she is less than a shadow in death. (CPP, 230)

A part of the house who frays the family line—"She never would have been one of the family, / She never wished to be one of the family"—she was the family member familial law could not control, the parasite inhabiting the house that stole away its valuable head and indulged in pleasurable circulations through expensive hotels. A "painted shadow" who has no proper name, she is even in death the figure whose physical body, whose essential substance, remains "permanently *missing*." Her interference disturbs with unsolvable difference the House of Monchensey and disperses its authority. No family reunion would be complete without her, but any reunion would be disrupted by her. Her murder is the practical solution—a forceful exclusion of difference—that might allow the family reunion to take place. It is therefore not surprising that, when Amy describes the wife's death as "a blessed relief," she speaks with the same will to overpower difference that had marked her desire to annul time. As Mary admits, "I believed that Cousin Amy / I almost believed it—had killed her by willing" (CPP, 230, 229, 245).

Harry's desire for his wife's death reflects a similar will to have closure, to exclude difference and route waywardness. When he finds himself without direction in the "crowded desert," he observes that one thinks to escape the wandering in the desert, and therefore to arrive at a promised homeland, by violence.

It was only reversing the senseless direction
For a momentary rest on the burning wheel
The cloudless night in the mid-Atlantic
When I pushed her over. (CPP, 235)

In both of these cases, the will to have closure, to delimit difference and wandering, is expressed in a will to commit violence, particularly the violent expulsion and murder of the figure of insistent difference. Agatha recalls Harry's father thinking of "How to get rid of [Harry's] mother" (CPP, 274). As Harry describes it, memory, unlike the difference-producing memory of Eliot's dissertation and more like the mediating device of *Murder*, is a type of violent forgetting of difference, a violence that is itself a will to have closure. He speaks of Wishwood:

I thought it was a place
Where life was substantial and simplified—
But the simplification took place in my memory. (CPP, 247)

The idea of the simple, the substantial, the individualized, and the routed is the result of a practical and willful domestication of wandering and play. When Mary and Harry were children, they played in the "wilderness," a place surrounding a hollow tree (CPP, 248). The tree recalls the linearity of the family tree, a figure of the familial origin and its subsequent branchings, which point back to their original root as to a paternal authority. But here, the tree is hollow, lacking in lawful authority, and thus the space surrounding the tree is indeed a wilderness, a place of the waywardness of wandering and the openness of unrestricted play. Its organizing root is already inhabited by a parasite that has eaten it away from the inside. (Stevens' "wilderness" in "Anecdote of the Jar" surrounds a similarly problematic artifact: the "jar" whose "dominion" is interrupted by the very fact of its placement as a willfully imposed point of order [CP, 76].)

The closure of the wilderness—the practical solution to the problem of difference—is ultimately interfered with by the artifice of its construction. Harry observes that "It's absurd that one's only memory of freedom / Should be a hollow tree in a wood by the river" (CPP, 248). That memory, however, recalls an originally unrestricted play prior to the imposition of a law—prior, that is, to the domestication of the space of play into a monumental blockhouse. The figure of the blockhouse recalls Stevens' difference-collapsing statue of General du Puy and Nietzsche's observation that man has a "powerful genius for architecture" with which he succeeds in "piling up an infinitely complex dome of ideas on a movable foundation and as it were on running water."[12] Like Nietzsche's "great edifice of ideas," which ignores the differences that constitute the ideas it builds upon, the blockhouse is constructed by a difference-obscuring will to power.

> The wilderness was gone,
> The tree had been felled, and a neat summer-house
> Had been erected, 'to please the children.' (CPP, 248)

Through this will to power and the supplemental edifice it constructs, the field of unrestricted play is translated into a proper summerhouse: difference is interpreted and transformed into the rigidity of an Apollonian idea. But like Apollo finally speaking with the contradictory language of Dionysus, or poetic meaning finally

12. Friedrich Nietzsche, *The Philosophy of Nietzsche*, ed. Geoffrey Clive (New York, 1965), 509.

repeating the interfering noise of music, this construction project, like Stevens' "later reason," only takes the place of the differences it obscures but cannot exclude.

The interferences in the House of Monchensey and the tropical prodigality of the North point toward another waywardness central to *The Family Reunion*—the irreducible waywardness of language. Throughout the play, language is described as a wandering of trope, as a detour through metaphor away from the punctual identity of a topic. For example, Harry can never speak plainly of his experiences; rather, he can do so only by parasitizing an analogous language.

> I am not speaking
> Of my own experience, but trying to give you
> Comparisons in a more familiar medium. (CPP, 234)

Topos here emerges only along with a declination or turn, a *tropos* that interferes with it but without which it can never be spoken. Every appeal to the true topic can thus take place only as a re-deployment of this constituting difference and of the relationship in which both *topos* and *tropos* emerge differentially.

> This is what matters, but it is unspeakable,
> Untranslatable:
> I talk in general terms
> Because the particular has no language. (CPP, 235)

No language emerges without this essential heterogeneity, for the topic has no language proper to it. There are, in other words, only dialects with no mother tongue, only differences with no resolving core of propriety. The abstractions of language make a difference only with respect to each other, always distinguishing themselves, like Stevens' representational clouds or Nietzsche's Nephelococcygiac ideas, from the concrete identity of a topic.

> Do you think that I believe what I said just now?
> That was only what I should like to believe.
> I was talking in abstractions: and you answered in abstractions.
> (CPP, 268)

This language describes a differential space of incommensurable abstractions that insists upon difference and disturbs the figure of closure that is the family reunion itself.

There is thus in this language a noise that cannot be excluded.

The characters' speeches never express the clear self-consistency of a topic, for as Harry notes twice in the play, "Everything is true in a different sense." Language emerges only as the recording of that difference, as a "whispering just out of earshot" that can never be quite silenced. The echo of the trope parasitizes the topic, but it is only as host to the parasite of trope—as the voice interrupted by the unfilterable noise of an echo—that a topic is ever addressed. What is suggested by the echo is the impossibility of producing an adequate explanation for the differences language insistently redeploys, for it is precisely the solution to the problem of difference figured by the verb *to explain* (*ex* + *planus*: to level or flatten out the irregularities or differences in a surface) that echoing noise disturbs. It is this endless disturbance that initially frustrates Harry. "But how can I explain, how can I explain to *you*? / You will understand less after I have explained it" (CPP, 235, 275, 250, 234). Explanations redeploy the noise they were intended to filter out of a "moment of clarity"; the lucid moment, in which the topic is plainly stated, is perpetually deferred.

> There are certain points I do not yet understand:
> They will be clear later. I am also convinced
> That you only hold a fragment of the explanation. (CPP, 236)

Thus the metaphoric language of explanation can never speak beyond the detour of its own speech. "In this world," says Agatha, the reason for Harry's eventual departure, the very *topos* of significance or center of the play, "is inexplicable, the resolution is in another" (CPP, 284). When it speaks, language does so only to articulate the absence of explanation and hence to redeploy its essential heterogeneity from a law of resolution.

> I can only speak
> So you may not think I conceal an explanation,
> And to tell you that I would have liked to explain. (CPP, 280)

As *The Family Reunion* repeatedly suggests, the resolving *topos* of the play and of language, the other world parasitized by repeated incorrect explanations, can appear only as the effects these mistaken explanations have on each other, as the interference points between one explanation and another. The resolution of these differing explanations is never simply present in the world of explanations, which has no core of self-consistent truth that would allow us to decide upon the ultimate correctness of any explanation. In the language of *The Family Reunion*, as in the history of Becket's death, there are a multiplicity of explanations, of interpretations, with no neutral point of resolution and no posted observer-elect. As Amy observes, this deficiency is essential to the declarations of speech.

> It is only because of what you do not understand
> That you feel the need to declare what you do.
> There is more to understand: hold fast to that
> As the way to freedom. (CPP, 236)

This differential freedom, however, repeatedly interferes with the play's desire for closure and reunion. As Amy desires the annihilation of the differences engendered by space and time, so the Chorus desires the satisfaction of an explanation that can account for noise and not itself repeat it.

> Any explanation will satisfy:
> We only ask to be reassured
> About the noises in the cellar
> And the window that should not have been open. (CPP, 243)

The Chorus wishes for the comforting tyranny of a divine writing, of an authoritative script that accounts for all of them. "Why do we feel embarrassed, impatient, fretful, ill at ease, / Assembled like amateur actors who have not been assigned their parts?" This desire runs in the family and extends to Harry himself, who chafes over the fact that he does not "know the words in which to explain" his leaving but who nevertheless feels "an overwhelming need for explanation." His need recalls Stevens' human wish for a language unparasitized by noise and difference. Like the rest of the family, Harry blindly desires a routed language whose explanatory detours will end in a return to a home of truth instead of the perpetually homeless heterogeneity of the trope. "Oh, there *must* be another way of talking / That would get us somewhere," that would place us in the proximity of a punctual *topos* (CPP, 231, 280, 259, 269). He expresses the wishful thinking of Eliot the theologian, but the articulation of this desire redeploys the difference that constitutes both the action and the language of *The Family Reunion*.

In this play, the metaphor of sight, like the figure of music in much of Eliot's criticism, seems to circumvent the irreducible differences of language by appearing to be the neutral medium of explanation, the sense through which the unmediated perception of truth in its unparasitized purity can be achieved. Mary, for example, speaks of the certainty of unmediated sight.

> I haven't much experience,
> But I see something now which doesn't come from tutors
> Or from books, or from thinking, or from observation. (CPP, 250)

In short, she asserts that she sees the true "something" betrayed by language and books. In a repetition of the conventional Platonic metaphor, what Mary sees appears as the light of the sun, a punctual lucidity she opposes to what she believes to be Harry's self-blinding declination from the *topos* of light and truth.

> You deceive yourself
> Like the man convinced that he is paralysed
> Or like the man who believes that he is blind
> While he still sees the sunlight. (CPP, 251)

Mary thus appears as the prophet of "singing and light," the observer-elect whose unmediated vision gives her insight into the purity of the truth itself.

Like Mary, Agatha also privileges the sense of sight. Speaking to Mary about Harry's return and its consequences, she affirms, "I see more than this, / More than I can tell you, more than there are words for," thus emphasizing the ability of sight to overcome the limitations of words. Finally, Harry himself praises the apparent immediacy of sight over the mediacy of language. "You can't know why I'm going. You have not seen / What I have seen" (CPP, 246, 287). For Harry, seeing is not only believing, it is neutral and accurate explanation.

> If I tried to explain, you could never understand:
> Explaining would only make a worse understanding;
> Explaining would only set one farther away from you.
> There is only one way for you to understand
> And that is by seeing. (CPP, 250)

Sight, like music, is believed to succeed where language fails. Both presumably aspire to the truth, but where linguistic explanation always bears the noise that interferes with truth, sight can coldly delineate it. Sight is the overcoming of the difference of language; sight closes its parasitizing detours.

Or does it? At this point, a certain interference can be traced in sight itself. What takes place at the moment of sight, which these characters have asserted to be the moment of insight? As Harry observes,

> . . . the eye adjusts itself to a twilight
> Where the dead stone is seen to be batrachian,
> The aphyllous branch ophidian. (CPP, 249)

The pupil turns not to focus upon a single point of light, a central sun, but upon an impasse, a difference in its own perception. The strange final two lines of the above quotation mark this interruption in the apparent neutrality of sight. The verb *is seen to be,* like the many *as if*'s in Stevens, opens the difference of metaphor within sight itself, which sees the dead stone and the aphyllous branch only as sites of difference, as the points at which neutral perception is interrupted by the perception of a trope. This perceptual moment is like sight in Stevens' "Description Without Place," which is never neutral but always makes a difference in what is seen, a difference that is the irreducible intrusion of the eye or the local point of view (CP, 344, 400). Like language, sight in *The Family Reunion* is never neutral and therefore deploys the same parasitizing difference as linguistic explanation. Perception discloses interference and difference, and the time of the eye is twilight, the margin that is not simply the time of the sun's presence nor simply the time of its absence, but rather the complicated time when darkness and light overlap and interrupt each other. It is these "flickering intervals of light and darkness," these moments "without purpose and without principle of conduct," that the eye records. Like language, which traces the declination between *topos* and *tropos* and the mutually parasitizing relationship in which both are differentially constituted, the eye sees the *clinamen* that constitutes both the seen and the unseen. "Here and here and here—wherever I am not looking, / Always flickering at the corner of my eye." The supposedly neutral, self-consistent sight shows itself only as the point of interference and difference. It is an irradiated "glow upon the world, that never found its object," an endlessly differentiating radiation that cannot be reduced to a pinpoint, illuminating identity (CPP, 235, 250, 249).

Whereas Amy seeks to annul his endless differentiation by annihilating time and space, Agatha sees it as the necessary though circuitous path leading to the revelation of truth itself, as a detour

whose end is mystical illumination: "When the loop in time comes—
and it does not come for everybody— / The hidden is revealed, and
the spectres show themselves" (CPP, 229). The loop for Agatha is
the closed circle that, as Grover Smith points out, "brings divers
times together, the ghosts of Christmas past and the ghosts of
Christmas future." [13] It suggests the end of difference and the reconciliation of multiple private worlds—"We must try to penetrate the
other private worlds / Of make-believe and fear" (CPP, 268)—in an
appeal to a neutral "real."

> . . . the past is irremediable,
> Because the future can only be built
> Upon the real past. (CPP, 228)

The loop or circle is thus, for Agatha, the most direct route to this
"real"; indeed, the circle is only a complex variant of the line, is the
indirect but routed path to revelation. In the rune that ends Part I,
she expresses her desire for an end to unprincipled, enigmatic wandering in the resolution of the straight line.

> There are three together
> May the three be separated
> May the knot that was tied
> Become unknotted
> . . . .
> [May] The eye of the day time
> And the eye of the night time
> Be diverted from this house
> Till the knot is unknotted
> The crossed is uncrossed
> And the crooked is made straight. (CPP, 257)

The desired denouement will come when proper linearity or lineage
is restored—when, that is, differences are connected to and controlled by a currently missing present: "I can guess about the past
and what you mean about the future; / But a present is missing,
needed to connect them" (CPP, 272). The final purpose of the loop
of time is for Agatha the redemption of the differences it has engendered. As in a similar via negativa that William Spanos traces in
Four Quartets, Agatha, unlike Amy, seeks "not to annul time but to

13. Grover Smith, Jr., *T. S. Eliot's Poetry and Plays: A Study in Sources and Meaning* (Chicago, 1956), 205.

redeem it, to fill the gaps between the traces, thus *verifying* the original absolute: the privileged, the authorizing, status of the Incarnation, the Word made Flesh." [14]

Agatha appears in the play as a compelling force of closure that seeks to account for difference by revealing the transcendent absolute to which all differences ultimately point. Harry describes her as the perfect source of all explanation.

I think I see what you mean,
Dimly—as you once explained the sobbing in the chimney
The evil in the dark closet, which they said was not there,
Which they explained away, but you explained them. (CPP, 237)

But like sight, Agatha herself redeploys the difference she comes to close. One of the critical moments of the play occurs when Agatha steps into the empty window embrasure, the "blank dark space of the French window at the back of the stage," the space already vacated by the Eumenides. [15] Her words, like Becket's in *Murder,* come as supplements to the silence of the Eumenides and explain the curse figured by these spectres. But this articulation, which occupies the space of the Eumenides only when that space has been left vacant, is far from simple. Agatha's explanation arises in the empty space of the embrasure, and although it comes to fill the gap from which the presence of its topic (the Eumenides) is missing, it nevertheless articulates and draws attention to the vacancy of the space it fills with words. A moment (like that of sight) of revelation deferred, it redeploys the essential heterogeneity of language by which the figure of the closed loop of time undergoes a knotty interruption.

And what of the central figures of the play, the Eumenides? Carol Smith observes that they allow unmediated access to the "real," because "to those who are permitted to view them they are more real than the illusions which the world imposes." [16] Although they appear to be signs of an ultimate reality transcending the local illusions of the world, the Eumenides nevertheless interfere with the self-consistency of reality and interrupt the patterned circularity of

14. William V. Spanos, "Hermeneutics and Memory: Destroying T. S. Eliot's *Four Quartets,*" *Genre,* XI (Winter, 1978), 539.
15. Bodkin, *Quest for Salvation,* 6.
16. Carol H. Smith, *T. S. Eliot's Dramatic Theory and Practice: From Sweeney Agonistes to The Elder Statesman* (Princeton, 1963), 129.

issuance and return figured by a family reunion. In their inter-
ferences can be traced an affirmation of difference that disturbs
Amy's will to overpower difference, that repeats a more radically
Nietzschean Will to Power.

> The will, in Will to Power, is not of the order of representation: will and
> power are not to be conceived in terms of psychic and physical. The will,
> in Will to Power, is the differential element of force. Difference is enacted
> not in a reiteration of the same, but in the self-affirmation of a force exer-
> cised against another force. A will commands; it affirms itself. For
> Nietzsche, profoundly anti-Hegelian, that does not mean that it compre-
> hends the other, assimilates, appropriates the non-self. For a will to af-
> firm itself is rather for it to affirm its difference.[17]

The will to overpower reiterated by both Amy and Agatha is a will
to have closure, to suppress difference in the re-presentation of the
same, but it is a force that emerges only along with the resisting
interference of another. This resistance is repeated by the Eumenides.

Harry gets his first sense of the Eumenides in "the sweet, sickly
tropical night," in the tropology of the South that interferes so disruptively in the topology of the North (CPP, 232). The Eumenides
parasitically inhabit any apparent closure, most noticeably in the
ancestral book of the family history. In an image directly related to
the Eumenides, the Chorus describes the desecration of history, of
the house, and of the book itself.

> . . . the wings of the future darken the past, the beak and
>   claws have desecrated
> History. Shamed
> The first cry in the bedroom, the noise in the nursery, mutilated
> The family album, rendered ludicrous
> The tenant's dinner, the family pic-nic on the moors. Have torn
> The roof from the house, or perhaps it was never there.
> And the bird sits on the broken chimney. (CPP, 256–57)

The family album, the book of the father and his lineage, is muti-
lated by the interference that occurs within it, for the appearance of
the Eumenides within that history recalls the violence against the
father, the declination from a controlling principle of conduct, that
opens familial history itself. In the Eumenides is recalled not only
the authority of the father, the supposed head of the family, but also

17. Alphonso Lingis, "The Will to Power," in David B. Allison (ed.), *The New
Nietzsche: Contemporary Styles of Interpretation* (New York, 1977), 41.

the original decapitation of that head and the dispersal of familial authority. In Greek legend the Eumenides have their origin in the blood of the father's severed genitals, and thus the "family album," the genealogical story of lineage and of the family's linear descent from its fathering root, is simultaneously the story of the castrating interference that frays the genealogical line out of which the family is originally constituted. It is the story of the productive and originating deployment of difference: of the host and the parasite; of law and declination, *topos* and *tropos*, meaning and music, message and noise.[18]

The "differential element of force" is incarnated in the Eumenides. Harry speaks of reconciliation as a falling, as a return to a ground of stasis and uniformity. "Everything tends toward reconciliation / As the stone falls, as the tree falls" (CPP, 275). The Eumenides redeploy difference, however, by preventing such an entropic, reductive falling into place.

> I thought foolishly
> That when I got back to Wishwood, as I had left it,
> Everything would fall into place. (CPP, 272)

Harry's return home only begins again the wandering of his history, a wandering whose closure on a reconciling *topos* is indefinitely deferred by the differentiating force figured by the Eumenides: "the last apparent refuge, the safe shelter, / That is where one meets them. That is the way of spectres." At the "still point of the turning world," the "quiet place" of reconciliation, lies the interference, the "stirring underneath the air," the differential force that cannot be finally explained and put to rest (CPP, 280, 119, 278).

Like musical dissonance, the Eumenides disturb the simplicity of harmony, of any Apollonian illusion of boundaries, for they represent a pure difference that, like error in Eliot's dissertation, resists simple location.

> Were they simply outside,
> I might escape somewhere, perhaps. Were they simply inside
> I could cheat them perhaps with the aid of Dr. Warburton—(CPP, 269)

Neither inside nor outside, the Eumenides disturb the boundary that distinguishes inside from outside and deploy the identity of each as a problem. With the appearance of the Eumenides, the spa-

18. Apollodorus, *The Library*, trans. Sir James George Frazer (London, 1921), 5.

tial categories of inside and outside lose their meaning, and their interference with each other negates any ultimate justification by which they can be coldly delineated. What the Eumenides emphasize is the effect the inside has on the outside (and vice versa), the overlapping or interfering relationship in which neither has a privileged identity, but in which both are constituted differentially.

The Eumenides, then, deploy difference as a productive force. This positive interpretation of difference is similar to the one prevalent in Eliot's dissertation, though it clashes noticeably with the sacramental hermeneutics of *Murder in the Cathedral*. Willfully obscured in *Murder* and, for that matter, at the end of *The Waste Land*, insistent difference is tentatively reaffirmed in *The Family Reunion*. Harry's reevaluation of the role of the Eumenides signals this alteration of Eliot's perception of difference. Initially, the Eumenides are vengeful pursuers that deny Harry any rest, but they become guides who direct him back to his wandering life in the desert. Thus Harry learns that his life's business depends on a joyfully unfulfilled desire.

> And now I know
> That my business is not to run away, but to pursue,
> Not to avoid being found, but to seek. (CPP, 280)

Spanos has also noticed this alteration in Eliot's acknowledgment, in *Four Quartets*, of the "old poetics as a broken instrument." "The 'goal' is no longer to arrive, to achieve closure wilfully, to return, with a finality that liberates him (and the reader) from time, to an absolute beginning, a beginning which is simultaneously an end, *arche*-and-*telos*, alpha-and-omega. It is closer to being the more modest one of retrieving or repeating beginnings in the sense of remembering *in and for the present* what the recollective imagination as Will to Power overlooks and forgets: the open-ended temporality or historicity of being." [19] In *The Family Reunion*, it is Harry who begins again by redeploying the difference of an earlier beginning: "At the beginning, eight years ago, / I felt, at first, that sense of separation" (CPP, 272). Characteristic of these beginnings, like those celebrated in Stevens' "Notes," is not the static identity of a punctual origin, a topical core or a family home, but an energetically differentiating aberration.

19. Spanos, "Hermeneutics and Memory," 550.

> . . . What you call the normal
> Is merely the unreal and the unimportant.
> I was like that in a way, so long as I could think
> Even of my own life as an isolated ruin,
> A casual bit of waste in an orderly universe.
> But it begins to seem just part of some huge disaster,
> Some monstrous mistake and aberration
> Of all men, of the world, which I cannot put in order. (CPP, 268)

Aberrant difference is affirmed in *The Family Reunion* as the essential force that constitutes the world and all men and interferes with the theological, human wish for a "normal," orderly, Apollonian universe.

This difference is also an essential part of poetic drama. Eliot's early essay on "The Possibility of a Poetic Drama" reflects on drama's beginning in difference. "The moment an idea has been transferred from its pure state in order that it may become comprehensible to the inferior intelligence it has lost contact with art. It can remain pure only by being stated simply in the form of general truth, or by being transmuted." That is, the pure idea is such only by parasitizing a language that is not its own. In this essential interference, the poetic drama, if it is to be art, thus begins as a *clinamen*, as the transmuting point at which its proper identity is transgressed or burglarized. In an attack earlier in the essay on Goethe's drama, Eliot notes that a creation of art should not embody a philosophy, but that it should "*replace* the philosophy" to the extent that the author's thought, which Eliot earlier situated at the origin of drama, is "sacrificed or consecrated . . . to make the drama" (SW, 68, 66, 64).

Eliot's affirmation of difference in *The Family Reunion* is not pure and simple, for, as in Stevens' ancient cycle of desire, there are in Eliot always two incommensurable hermeneutics, two intervening forces. His affirmation of difference emerges only with the interference of a desire for a core of identity, and vice versa. Expressing an Apollonian desire for meaningful and just boundaries, Eliot seeks to obscure the difference deployed in *The Family Reunion* in the 1951 essay "Poetry and Drama," in which he tries to account for the "deepest flaw of all" in the play. This flaw is an unresolvable aberration in the Eumenides. "We tried every possible manner of presenting them. . . . They never succeed in being either Greek goddesses or modern spooks." The result is that "we are left in a divided frame of mind, not knowing whether to consider the play the tragedy of the mother or the salvation of the son. The two situations are not reconciled." Eliot here wishes he could have established the proper identity of the Eumenides, whose resistance to categorization now seems to him not the essential energy of the play but rather a flaw that interferes with its success. But in spite of this essay's explicit will to overpower difference, in spite of its attempt to define difference as an unfortunate but potentially rectifiable mistake, *The Family Reunion* ultimately interprets any such will to closure as the will to death. The house, so closely aligned throughout the play with the will to overpower difference, finally, by becoming Amy's tomb, appears, like Stevens' monument to General du Puy, to be the site of death. Harry himself suggests the "folly" of the "instinct to return to the point of departure" and the unnaturalness of "this arresting of the normal change of things" (OPP, 90; CPP, 249, 247). Indeed, the very life of the house (like, ultimately, the life of the Chorus in *Murder*) and of its head depends upon the difference whose collapse spells death to both.

> Here the danger, here the death, here, not elsewhere:
> Elsewhere no doubt is agony, renunciation
> But birth and life. Harry has crossed the frontier
> Beyond which safety and danger have a different meaning
> And he cannot return. (CPP, 284)

The house reestablishes itself upon a figure of eccentric impropriety—John, the "satisfactory son"—while its proper authority (the rightful heir, the father's appointed son, the sun itself) appears there only along with the interference of a disguise. Harry's return in the play, the desired restoration of the head of the family, is only a metaphoric return; he does not take command of Wishwood, but returns to it only as a guest lodging in another hotel in an endless chain (CPP, 286, 261). The circle of family reunion thus closes only with a return of trope and a redeployment of difference.

> Look, I do not know why,
> I feel happy for a moment, as if I had come home.
> . . . .
> . . . This is like an end. (CPP, 275)

It closes only to repeat the noisy dissonance of insubstantial forces, of multiple, powerless phantoms (Harry says that he has been "wounded in a war of phantoms, / Not by human beings—they have no more power than I" [CPP, 276]) whose interferences constitute the drama's life.

The "curse" of difference is thus both affirmed and obscured in *The Family Reunion* and in its language. Mary finally suggests that this curse is a kind of writing inscribed in everything, an aberrant, excessive, and parasitic mark that interferes with the simple identity of things.

> A curse is written
> On the under side of things
> Behind the smiling mirror
> And behind the smiling moon. (CPP, 292)

For Mary, and often for Eliot, difference is a curse, a frustrating interference inhabiting all things, but in *The Family Reunion* it is also the force essential to the constitution of the world, of man, and of his language. In the repetition of this determining difference lies the *clinamen* of all beginnings. When *The Family Reunion* ends, it does so only with such a repetition.

> This way the pilgrimage
> Of expiation
> Round and round the circle
> Completing the charm
> So the knot be unknotted
> The crossed be uncrossed
> The crooked made straight
> And the curse be ended
> By intercession. (CPP, 293)

Agatha's rune bespeaks an Apollonian desire for the end of the curse of difference, for the overcoming of the aberrant. At the same time, however, it is the recipe for that difference's redeployment. For the curse can be ended only by intercession, only by the repetition of a differentiating interference.

The parasites that inhabit identity are many in Eliot. The Eumenides, burglars, and echoes are only the locally significant representatives of a general interference that intrudes upon and interrupts all perceptions, cognitions, and assertions in Eliot's works. These interferences redeploy difference insistently, without containment; they are the curse written on things Mary describes in *The Family Reunion,* or the curse written in history from which Eliot seeks relief in the sacramental hermeneutics of *Murder in the Cathedral.* The curse suggests that all things, all ideas, all words, have a fundamentally contradictory being, that all things are sites of differences, tensive balances of incommensurable significances with no cognitive core. Within the unified message, as part of its constituting condition, is the random noise that interferes with its identity. Amy's will to overpower expresses a desire to eliminate the differential complement from identity. But since the curse of difference constitutes the differential life of all things, the desire for an uninterrupted message is the desire for death. In Eliot's dissertation, error has no home and cannot be contained, and difference is essential. In *The Family Reunion,* the curse of difference is also the breath of life.

Stevens' writings have their own parasitic echoes; the irreducible difference of the sea and of trope in "The Comedian as the Letter C" or the clashing forces of the auroras in their poem are sites of difference in which incommensurable forces insistently intrude upon each other and exist only as those intrusions. In the beginning was the noise; at the origin is interference and difference. Identities in Stevens are always being produced, but as parasitized by interference. Meaningful ideals from which interference seems to be tuned out, identities nevertheless interrupt themselves with the noise of their incidental and improvisational being, their status as practical, methodological solutions to the problem of difference. The will to overpower difference eternally returns in both Eliot and Stevens as the problem of difference redeployed by the improvised solution. Difference interferes with the catalepsy of identity (it is interference and noise in the unified message or text), but it is the parasite that animates the body of poetry.

Four
Echoes and Noise

In a letter written to José Rodriguez Feo in 1948, Wallace Stevens describes two styles of reading poetry. Characterizing his own state of mind about poetry as "very susceptible," and feeling himself to be in danger of picking up something unconsciously from other poets, Stevens writes, "In order not to run that danger I don't read other peoples' poetry at all." Or, he writes further, when he does, he reads that poetry only "at the finger tips, so to speak." He opposes this style of reading, which consciously refuses to plumb the depths of poetry by remaining only on its superficial surface, to the style in which "most people read it [poetry]"—by "listening for echoes because the echoes are familiar to them. They wade through it the way that a boy wades through water, feeling with his toes for the bottom" (LWS, 575). Whereas Stevens reads by lightly treading water or by floating in poetry's sea of words and reading its surface with his fingertips, these people read by searching in its watery language for a "bottom" of literal substance that, like a meaty incarnation of some ultimate meaning, would be the ground upon which they could safely walk. From this neutral ground they could completely explain the shifting differences and account for the multiple currents of poetry's words. For Stevens, this wading in the river of poetry suggests a style of reading that can pass through poetry's flowing verbiage only by finding the solid core that supports and shapes it. It cautiously wades; it does not risk the freedom of floating or of being carried away by poetry's metaphoric tides and currents.

This hermeneutics, however, ultimately encounters interference and noise, for as Stevens observes, "The echoes are the bottom." On one hand the figure of the bottom suggests a stable ground discoverable at the most profound limits of poetry's depths; on the other hand the characterization of that bottom as "echoes" raises some perplexing problems for those who would wade through poetry. *Echoes* here suggests influence, the appearance of another's voice in one's own poetry, and Stevens reflects a certain anxiety about such influence when he writes, "It is not so much that it [his style of reading] is a way of being oneself as it is a way of defeating people who look only for echoes and influences" (LWS, 575). Echoes, in other words, multiply the voice in poetry; an echo is a complementary, parasitic, and interfering overvoice that repeats what is spoken as though it came from a different source. Far from revealing a determinable and substantial poetic bottom or a single, univocal identity that grounds poetry's flood of words and voices, the echo suggests a polyphony of voices in which identity can only be a problem.

This echoing bottom can be characterized by the figure of the ellipse, the circle constituted by the interference of two complementary focal points. According to Stevens, poetry's bottom is by definition elliptical; there is always the interference of a radically incommensurable voice, center, or bottom that disturbs the ground upon which the wading reader so securely walks. This multiplicity of bottoms means that there can be no core of determinate meaning or significance, for no matter where the reader takes his stand, the ground below splits into two and is constituted by this essential difference. The echo interrupts every site of resolution, every bottom, and washes away its firm security even as the reader locates it in poetry's depths. Thus poetry's bottom is elliptical in another sense: since there are always too many bottoms, the bottom itself is what the sea of poetry always cites as a lacuna. The elliptical and perplexing nature of poetry's bottom finally defeats the terrestrial reader, for the bottom he finds to walk on, the foundation upon which he grounds his reading, dissolves into a polyphonous echoing that leaves him, finally, at sea.

This is exactly where we find Crispin, in "The Comedian as the Letter C"—swimming in a polyphonous sea and searching for a new ground to replace the "lost terrestrial," a bottom of profound security that can stem the inscrutable "verboseness" of poetry's watery words (CP, 28). "The Comedian" recounts a voyage of cancellations and displacements in which Crispin sails from Bordeaux to Yucatan to Havana to Carolina, journeying from one ground, one poetic bottom, to another and another, only to have each new terra firma redeploy the multiplicity of difference that interferes with its univocal identity and returns the voyager and the poem itself to an unstemmable polyphony. In his search for poetry's bottom, Crispin can be seen as a figure of a sacramental, Eliotic quester (Pearce suggested that "The Comedian" is meant as "a kind of reply to 'The Waste Land'").[1] It is this hermeneutical style, which seeks to interpret differences as the signs of an underlying profundity, that Stevens' water treading interferes with, and the significance of Crispin's sacramental journey is disturbed by the irony that overwrites the entire poem. Stevens writes Crispin's romantic quest for poetry's insoluble *ding an sich* only to parasitize it, only, that is, to interrupt it and deploy it as a problem. In this sense, then, the poem repeats the disturbing interferences that characterize each of Crispin's landfalls, and thus the poem is, as Stevens has described it, "antimythological," a parasitic erosion of the myth of poetry's profundity and of the essence of univocal meaning that lies within the depths of its words (LWS, 778). Crispin always finds another land in "The Comedian as the Letter C," but those lands, like all poetic bottoms, echo the polyphonic difference that washes over and dissolves their literal identity. It is the force of this echoing interference that overtakes all poetry's notas, words, and assertions, and that leaves Crispin, and the wading reader who would "feel with his toes" for a core of profound meaning, no place to stand.

Crispin's journey through oceans of words begins with a displacement of the "mythology of self," the ground of a "wordy, watery age" whose center was Bordeaux and whose episteme is the poem's first nota: "man is the intelligence of his soil." This mythology, a poetic ground that is now a "lost terrestrial," is "blotched out beyond unblotching," indelibly blemished by an interfering mark (like the curse written "On the underside of things" in *The Family Reunion*) that cancels its significance and washes away its "snug hibernal." Crispin's poetic passage, therefore, begins at sea with a

---

1. Roy Harvey Pearce, *The Continuity of American Poetry* (Princeton, 1961), 424.

memory not simply of land but of that land's dissolution into the polyphony of the sea, of the splitting of univocality into the differences of "clickering syllables" and "multitudinous tones." It is a beginning like the one recounted in the Monchensey family album, which recalls the family's beginning in the dismemberment of its father. And it is a beginning like the one written of in the opening canto of "Notes toward a Supreme Fiction," where the invented world of poetry is opened by the differentiation of "us and our images" from a "heaven" that can only be recalled by the imagination as an impossible time always before the beginning (CP, 381). "The Comedian," like "Notes," begins with the imperfection or interference that separates poetry from a referential core and releases the flooding verboseness of its incommensurable figures. Crispin is "washed away" by this verbal magnitude. No longer able to wade through the proliferation of words by walking on the secure, grounding bottom of the self, which can no longer be interpreted as the site of reconciling identity and univocality but is blotched by an interfering difference, Crispin must tread water until he can find a new ground from which to "stem verboseness in the sea."

It is the "veritable ding an sich" that Crispin seeks to substitute for the perplexing insignificance of the self. In classically Stevensian terms, Crispin supplements the "blotched out" and "split up" imagination with the literal bottom of reality, the substantial ground that will hold firm and resolve poetry's polyphony. Crispin's move is like Eliot's in *Murder,* whose supplementation of a sacramental perspective on Becket's death is intended to resolve the polyphony of historical interpretations in an ahistorical reality beyond interpretation. And yet the "starker, barer world" Crispin desires and believes he confronts redeploys the same blotch, the same interference, that canceled the mythology of the self. For while the *ding an sich* suggests the thing itself unadorned by the "distortion[s] of romance," or the bottom of profound literality underlying the watery fictions of poetry, this suggestion is complicated by its description as "gaudy, gusty panoply" and "caparison of wind and cloud": "something given to make whole among / The ruses that were shattered by the large." The thing itself bears an interference, an incommensurable and "unavoidable shadow," that irreducibly doubles its significance as both disclosed reality and as the ornamental sign or covering for something else, something as insubstantial and variable as "wind and cloud" (CP, 30, 29). Perplexed by this interrupting difference is the insoluble security of the *ding an sich,* which, like the earlier ground of the self, turns out to be a blotched figure, a site of difference, the source of an echoing noise. The *ding an sich,* like the bottom irreducibly doubled in an echo, is duplicitously folded back on itself; inhabiting it is a complicating extra significance that is at once the condition of its appearance and the noise that interferes with its identity. To unfold this complication, to banish noise in an appeal to a profundity the reader can securely base a reading on, leaves only an elliptical gap.

Like Harry in *The Family Reunion,* Crispin wanders in a tropical world, and his first landfall, Yucatan, is a noisy bottom for the verboseness of poetry and words. In this tropical paradise, Crispin senses an

> . . . elemental fate,
> And elemental potencies and pangs,
> And beautiful barenesses as yet unseen. (CP, 31)

For this "indigenous dew" he proposes a natural, intrinsic poetic style, "an aesthetic tough, diverse, untamed . . . Green barbarism turned paradigm." But Yucatan is a "land of snakes," and Crispin's verses of its "fabulous . . . earth" come "so intertwined with serpent-kin encoiled / Among the purple tufts, the scarlet crowns" that the

> . . . earth was like a jostling festival
> Of seeds grown fat, too juicily opulent,
> Expanding in the gold's maternal warmth. (CP, 32)

The earth here echoes the polyphony of the sea in which Crispin first found himself adrift. It suggests a fabulous subject, an essential, univocal topic for the words of Crispin's fables, but a topic in which figures of mastery and authority ("purple tufts" and "scarlet crowns") are disturbed by an opulence (a "serpent-kin") that in one of the many senses of this image bears the poison that contaminates paradise and begins the exile of man and his images. Thus the earth, like the sea itself and its elliptical, echoing bottom, tropes a difference not controlled by Crispin's quill or reduced to his catechism. Having apparently touched the bottom of poetry's marine verboseness by landing in tropical Yucatan, Crispin nevertheless continues to tread water in a polyphonous sea of differences in which the univocal topic can be heard only along with the noisy interference of trope.

He is forced, finally, to take refuge from this tropical polyphony behind the façade of the cathedral, to retreat, like Eliot in *Murder,* to the sacramental hermeneutics figured in "Connoisseur of Chaos" as the bishop's books, which once "resolved the world" by proving that "opposite things partake of one" and that differences are spoken by one divine voice. This sacramental rhetoric is not noticeably different from the poetic style figured by the now-dissolved Triton, and although "Crispin was too destitute to find / In any commonplace the sought-for aid," his kneeling "in the cathedral with the rest" is a retreat to the most commonplace figure of profundity, to the theological trope of a bottom already canceled in Triton and later dissolved by the announcement of "Connoisseur of Chaos" that "We cannot go back to that" (CP, 215).

What drives him to this retrograde façade—another protective panoply—is a watery onslaught, the storm that washes over Yucatan as a torrent proclaiming the span "Of force, the quintessential fact, the note / Of Vulcan" (CP, 33). This volcanic note is sounded again, much later, in the opening canto of "Esthétique du Mal," where Vesuvius reminds the writing poet of the pain that washes away the world-resolving security of the book of the sublime.

> . . . He could describe
> The terror of the sound because the sound
> Was ancient. He tried to remember the phrases . . .
> . . . .
> . . . His book
> Made sure of the most correct catastrophe.
> Except for us, Vesuvius might consume
> In solid fire the utmost earth and know
> No pain . . .
> . . . This is a part of the sublime
> From which we shrink. (CP, 314)

Joseph Riddel reads this volcanic note as a decentering force that overtakes the book and its orderly account of "nature and history as a fallenness": "With the end of the book of the sublime, the order of displacements, the hierarchy of signifieds, is radically disrupted." This disruption means that "the master term, that which might govern or center all the others, is brought into question, decentered—placed 'sous rature,' under erasure."[2] There is always, in

2. Joseph N. Riddel, "Metaphoric Staging: Stevens' Beginning Again at the 'End of the Book,'" in Frank Doggett and Robert Buttel (eds.), *Wallace Stevens: A Celebration* (Princeton, 1980), 309, 310.

other words, in any "master term" the incommensurable mark, the parasitizing significance, or the interference it cannot control. Such a term is the site of both hermeneutical law and declination, of proper order and burglary. Seen in this way, the "note of Vulcan" in "The Comedian" repeats the noise of difference that characterizes the polyphony of the sea and the disruptive, interfering echo of its bottom.

Crispin's search for a literality upon which to center or organize the drift of words takes him to the "marshy ground" of Carolina, a new world already awash in the watery, dissolving interferences figured by the sea and the Mexican torrent. Renouncing the "gemmy marionette" of "moonlight fiction," he "savored rankness like a sensualist," continuing a quest, like that of the Canon Aspirin in "Notes," for the insoluble ground of a reality uncomplicated by divagation or evasion, by words or poetry. Like many of Stevens' personae (Ozymandias, for example), Crispin desires contact with the "nude," the bottom that grounds the "poem of pure reality, untouched / By trope or deviation," with, in Peirce's terms, "meaning . . . stripped of [the] irrelevant clothing" of representations. But as Peirce suggests, "This clothing can never be stripped off; it is only changed for something more diaphanous."[3] And as Ozymandias later discovers, the naked bride appears only along with a fictive covering that interferes with her nakedness. Stevens writes in another poem that the nude always carries the "flag of the nude," the supplementary trope without which the nude, that which should be simply itself, never appears (CP, 34, 35, 471, 330). Similarly, Crispin's marshy Carolinian ground is dissolved by watery interferences. It is like the world Stevens writes of in the twenty-third canto of "The Man with the Blue Guitar":

> The world washed in his imagination,
> The world was a shore, whether sound or form
>
> Or light, the relic of farewells,
> Rock, of valedictory echoings,
>
> To which his imagination returned,
> From which it sped, a bar in space,
>
> Sand heaped in clouds, giant that fought
> Against the murderous alphabet. (CP, 179)

3. Charles Hartshorne and Paul Weiss (eds.), *Collected Papers of Charles Sanders Peirce* (8 vols.; Cambridge, 1960), I, 171.

This grounding rock echoes itself as a "relic of farewells," a phrase Stevens characterizes in a letter to Hi Simons in terms of the land and the sea: "Our imagination of or concerning the world so completely transformed it that, looking back at it, it was a true land's end. But the transformation having been effected, the imagination with its typical nostalgia for reality tried to go back to recover the world. It was not so much a remote land's end as something that changed its identity, denied its familiar intelligence" (LWS, 364).

Crispin's new nota, the founding rock of his colonial fabrication, redeploys the polyphonous transformations its affirmation was to command. Hinted at in the caution that doubles his "essential prose" as a "poem's guise," this difference is suggested by the very prominence of the nota (a term that means both to take note and to swim).[4] Its designation of the textual bottom, in other words, has an interfering echo (the command to swim), and this irreducible complication leaves Crispin where he has always been: at sea, swimming. His new nota—indeed, any nota, assertion, or profound literality that can be said to master the polyphony of poetry's words—is no more a bottom to the sea's verboseness, allowing one to wade securely through poetry's drifting tropes, than is the blotched one that opened the poem. Its reversal repeats the parasitizing imperfection that at once characterizes and interrupts any central assertion, any conceptual law, which must therefore be constituted only as inhabited by the declination that disturbs its identity and multiplies its significance. Whereas Crispin plans a colony (whose Greek root *kyklos* suggests a circle), a "family reunion" whose periphery is commanded by a single center, his "prose / More exquisite than any tumbling verse" discloses the elliptical and plural nature of all centers. His goal is to stem the bottomless drift of words by banishing the noisy "trash" of masquerade and counterfeit, in which the true is complicated with the false, the literal with the figurative, the text with the gloss, the central prose with the eccentric trope (CP, 39). Hence he provides the stage directions,

> Exit the mental moonlight, exit lex,
> Rex and principium, exit the whole
> Shebang. Exeunt omnes. (CP, 37)

But this quest "to make a new intelligence prevail . . . Related in romance to backward flights" and "contained in [its] afflatus the re-

---

4. Merle E. Brown, *Wallace Stevens: The Poem as Act* (Detroit, 1970), 59.

proach / That first drove Crispin to his wandering." The "monoto-nous babbling in our dreams" is a polyphonous babel of voices that multiplies to indeterminacy the dreams' controlling law, making those dreams at once "our dependent heirs" and "the heirs / Of dreamers buried in our sleep." For this reason "All dreams are vex-ing," and thus Crispin would expunge them and their noise and "drive away / The shadow of his fellows from the skies." But Triton, the figure of a "stale intelligence," was himself an "ancient Crispin." Thus this expunging, the asserted reduction of watery tropes to the bottom of an intelligence that is their profound significance, repeats in a new figure the "stale intelligence" it displaces (CP, 37, 39, 29). The polyphonous babbling resists its new law, and the "new intelli-gence" redeploys the same difference that disclosed the staleness of the old.

"The Comedian as the Letter C" provides the wading reader no place to stand that is not at once the trope of a bottom and a dis-torting interference. The search of Crispin for a grounding bottom, or of the reader for the security of a determinate and insoluble reso-lution to poetry's polyphony, traces an inevitable poetics of failure in which any asserted core of significance, any nota describing a grounding truth lying within the depths of poetry's verbal drift, also describes the echoing noise that inhabits and disturbs it. The "my-thology of self" bears this interfering blotch and so, finally, do the pronouncements of the realist who clings to the "surviving form," to the new text of reality that displaces with an inverted redeploy-ment the old language of the self. "For realist, what is is what should be," and thus the phenomenal *is*—the "plum that survives the poem"—appears both as a description of a reality beyond rhetoric and as a rhetorical prescription, since "shall or ought to be" echo in the *is*. The denouement, the unfolding of this entangled textual complication in a reading that would resolve it by plumbing its depths, must, like the casual balances of "Notes," ultimately seem "haphazard" (CP, 41, 40). Such denouements never disclose a secure bottom but rather suggest a random drift of methodologi-cally imposed metaphors, each of which redeploys and complicates the idea of disentangled literality. The unfolding of the poem's poly-phony, like the demythologizing of Triton, undoes not the divaga-tions and veiling guises of its tropes but rather the assertion that these differences hide a bottom or cognitive core that, if located, would provide the neutral ground of truth from which to definitively interpret the poem and stem its tide of words in a revelation of literal meaning. For Stevens "the echoes are the bottom," and any ground is insistently marshy and multiple. Crispin's Carolina cabin is indistinguishable from the remembered "lost terrestrial" of Bordeaux, and his tale's denouement, by returning him again to the already denounced "salad-beds" of the past, folds back on itself as another relic of the perpetual "farewells," of the essential exile and haphazard drift, of poetry. These grounding "salad-beds," however simple, echo with a perplexing interference, for in the roots of *salad* (from the Latin *sal,* meaning salt, and the Greek *hals,* suggesting both salt and sea) resonates the dissolving noise of the sea of trope. Crispin's journey, like Harry's, is a lateral drift between multiple localities, each of which is itself a site of interference, difference, and trope.

This noise also resounds in the "fertile main" that Crispin has supposedly pruned of its confusing "verboseness" with his doctrine of the "fecund minimum." The "fertile main," the poem's final figure of the substantial "plum" that survives the watery, polyphonous drift of its poems, echoes with multiple, incommensurable significations. Its suggests at once the mainland and the sea; the grounding bottom and its erosive interference; an energetic, constituting difference stemmed only figuratively by a methodological doctrine "concocted . . . from the rout." Like Eliot's "fragments . . . shored against my ruins" at the end of *The Waste Land* or the Apollonian illusion of identity and noncontradictory truth in Nietzsche, such a doctrinal law only draws our attention to the "rout" of differences that always comes first and that therefore echoes in any privileged construction or architecture of ideas (CP, 45; CPP, 50). "The same insoluble lump," disclosed to be the literality essential to each of Crispin's landfalls, splits like the sea into polyphony, redeploying the difference that interferes with the identity of the "same." Whereas on one hand the "insoluble lump" suggests the rocklike security of a profound identity that cannot be dissolved by poetry's watery words, on the other it outlines a complicated lump with no such bottom, an insoluble puzzle or perplexing statement that can never be reduced to a solution that would resolve it. The lump, then, names the fertile interference in which both resolution and dissolution, both identity and difference, are constituted. Its significance is essentially multiple and contradictory; it *is* the interfering echo that frustrates the reader's wish to wade through poetry on secure cognitive ground. Crispin's "proclamations of the pure" are interrupted by the "deluging onwardness" of their delivery in the same way that "The Comedian as the Letter C" is interfered with by the problem of its final question: "If the anecdote / Is false," if Crispin ends up

> . . . proving what he proves
> Is nothing, what can all this matter since
> The relation comes, benignly, to its end? (CP, 46)

Here is a watery assertion and cancellation resolved only by the poem's final, supplementary line—"So may the relation of every man be clipped"—in which Stevens cuts the Gordian knot of differential relations only by playing the role of Alexander, by clipping the poem's "inscrutable hair" in a "haphazard" denouement that is improvised and strictly practical (CP, 27). The intervention ends the poem the same way the intercession of Agatha's rune ends *The Family Reunion,* in an improvisation that redeploys a "deluging onwardness" of difference that leaves us, finally, where Crispin began: treading water, adrift in a verbal polyphony beyond the plumbing thrust of our critical baton.

The "quintessential fact" of words and writing disclosed in "The Comedian as the Letter C" turns out to be, like the fecund principle of "Notes" or the dissonant music inhabiting poetic meaning for Eliot, not a firm, resolving ground of literal truth underlying the drifting divagations of figuration and trope but rather a differentiating force that interrupts any asserted truth, any figure of a *ding an sich* literality readable within the figurations of writing. Always suggesting too much, always disclosing (within any critical reading that might account for the turns of trope by grounding them in a cognitive core of profound meaning) an additional center of reference that the reading cannot account for, words disturb reading as a hermeneutical act whose goal is to locate in a text the bottom that resolves, limits, centers, or masters and organizes its verbal flow.

This interference, the difference one fact makes to another in an endlessly differential field of multiple facts with no centrally neutral identity, is the quintessential characteristic of all facts and words. As Stevens suggests, no fact can be written without this interference, but no fact stands as a simple, neutral identity against it. The noise that both constitutes and distorts the message renders all facts of writing essentially unstable; it disturbs the literal identity presumed to underlie the differing metaphors of poetry even as it is itself another metaphor of such a cognitive core. It deploys, therefore, a difference that defeats the reader who would wade securely through a text by walking on a stable bottom of truth, a poisonous interference that marks such points of cognitive stability as accidental "balances that happen" or as the sites of an imposition of a methodological will to overpower differences (CP, 386). This interference point insists on the essential heterogeneity of truths and on their strictly local, differential significances.

This poison of interference is productively deployed in both Eliot and Stevens. It has no figure more apt than the serpent, which is central in Stevens' "The Auroras of Autumn." As Joseph Riddel has pointed out, there are "at least two . . . 'nests'" for the serpent in this poem's opening canto.[5] The first is a poetic nest of trope and figure.

> This is where the serpent lives. This is his nest,
> These fields, these hills, these tinted distances,
> And the pines above and along and beside the sea. (CP, 411)

This nest is "form gulping after formlessness," a physical "skin flashing to wished-for disappearances / And the serpent body flashing without the skin." But this nest, like Crispin's many landfalls, is overwritten by an interfering blotch, an extra significance that opens its reading as the "form" or "skin" of an ideal, formless serpent (the "master of the maze / Of body and air and forms and images") to an alternate, incommensurable reading as

> . . . another wriggling out of the egg,
> Another image at the end of the cave,
> Another bodiless for the body's slough. (CP, 411)

Does the nest, a verbose maze of tropes and figures, disclose in his formless absence the serpent that masters and grounds its labyrinthine body? Or does that body, like the meaning always missing (for Eliot) from Milton's mazes of sound, reveal only the presence of another image, another shadowy illusion, and therefore no master at all? These questions probe for a profound bottom grounding the flashing figures of poetry, but they disclose such a bottom as problematically elliptical and the poetic nest itself as a perplexing polyphony of incommensurable significances.

5. Riddel, "Metaphoric Staging," 333.

The second nest, however, is not the poisonously blotched one the canto first describes but an ideal one that exists elsewhere and that does not disturb with a question the presence of its mastering serpent. Rather, it seems to confirm his mastery; it is a nest in which we can actually "find the serpent" and not be caught in the labyrinthine interferences that disrupt the first nest. This nest, like the Wishwood that Amy desires but never attains, would be the site of the resolution of differences, a structure of "forms and images" that would rest securely on and represent without interference a cognitive core of meaning, an identity inhabiting its different images. But such a lucid text can be thought here only as deferred into a problematic future—"these lights may finally attain a pole." The qualifying "may" overwrites the assertion with a different possibility that they may not. The "may" traces an interference that cannot be discounted, an irreducible perplexity that characterizes even this figure of ideal representation. This, then, is the poison of the serpent, this canto's trope of a core of significance to the textual maze that "The Comedian" troped as the "verboseness of the sea." Within this trope of poetry's referential, resolving bottom lies as a condition for the trope's being written in the poem the constituting interference of the possibility of its being simply "another image at the end of the cave" (CP, 28). The serpent is a site of incommensurable significances that deploys difference by suspending any ultimate justification for either interpretation. This is the difference Eliot tries to close in *Murder in the Cathedral* and hesitantly affirms in *The Family Reunion*.

"The Auroras of Autumn," then, deploys its figure of the master as an insoluble problem. Rather than making us "sure of [the] sun" and thereby validating an ideal center of the textual universe, this figure breaks up the sun into what Riddel calls its "colorations," into the plurality of figures—"Black beaded on the rock, the flecked animal, / The moving grass, the Indian in his glade"—that is another perplexing textual maze (CP, 412).[6] There is, for this canto, no resolution to the labyrinth of poetry except another figure that is, like the world Crispin discovers, "the same insoluble lump" and, therefore, like the intervening rune that ends *The Family Reunion*, another redeployment of difference. The sun repeats the Platonic ideal of neutral literality and ideal truth, but the only sun that the serpent's meditations make us sure of turns out to be auroral in na-

6. *Ibid.*

ture—those multiple, enigmatic lights whose appearance marks a clash of electrical forces, a field of energy and interferences with no substantial essence or punctual site of illumination. Like the Eumenides, the auroras figure a pure, constituting difference without appeal to a core of identity, and thus, like the echoes that suggest the differential bottom of poetry, the auroras disturb the will to overpower differences figured by the Platonic sun. Michel Benamou touches on the disturbing energy of the auroras when he suggests that "l'aurore ["une source lumineuse non-centré"] offre en effet un provocation à la rêverie de l'origine. La lumière disséminée, la dissémination lumineuse, conduiront à rêver une autre dissémination, celle du Pere et du Logos, substituts symboliques du centre divin."[7] The poetic bottom in the Rodriguez Feo letter, Crispin's notas, and the sun of "The Auroras" each disclose the interference that intervenes in their apparent identities.

The auroras' differential force sweeps the poem's second canto as the boreal "gusts of great enkindlings" that blow through this poem's reenvisioning of Crispin's familial cabin, the final ground the searcher arrived at in his quest. The cabin had been full of personae Crispin took to be "four sure answerers" to the sea's inscrutability (CP, 413, 41, 412, 45). The cabin now "stands, / Deserted, on a beach," a nest emptied of everything but the signs of its perplexed and problematic past, the flowers that are

> Reminding, trying to remind, of a white
> That was different, something else, last year
> Or before, not the white of an aging afternoon. (CP, 412)

These signs recall the youthful past as a time that can only be remembered as an enigmatic maze of possibilities. The cabin, an edifice like Wishwood or the first canto's nest of forms and images that gulps after the formlessness of ideal identity, is thus another "relic of farewells," a "typical nostalgia"—"as by a custom or according to / An ancestral theme"—for a purely white past uncontaminated by the differential colorations of the present. But like the statue of General du Puy, this nostalgia repeats the difference that constitutes its past; the boreal winds blow through the cabin, multiplying

7. Michel Benamou, *L'Oeuvre—Monde de Wallace Stevens* (Lille, 1973), 348–49: "The auroras [a de-centered light source] in effect offer a provocation to the dream of the origin. Disseminated light, luminous dissemination, leads us to dream another dissemination, that of the Father and of Logos, symbolic substitutes for the divine center."

and disseminating its grounding significance like "sand across the floor." The canto ends not in the remembrance of this pure past but in the redeployment of the prismatically split colors of "frigid brilliances," in the redeployment of difference like that repeated by the Monchensey family album and by Stevens' "typical nostalgia for reality" (LWS, 364; CP, 412, 413).

The poison that interferes with the second canto's traditional figure of a pure past from which the present poem has fallen also disturbs the third canto's trope of the poetic bottom all wading readers search for—"the purpose of the poem" that supports the poetic edifice and "fills the room" of its "forms and images" with an essential profundity. But this figure of poetic "purpose," and thus of poetry as a polyphony of words ultimately resolved in a unified intentionality, "has grown old" and is another idea about poetry and metaphor that "we cannot go back to" (CP, 413, 215). This sign of grounding purpose and mastering significance can be written only along with the noise of its dissolution and destruction. Like the meaning of poetry in Eliot, the purpose of the poem in Stevens emerges as the habitation of a parasite, as a point of irreducible interference. This constituting interference deploys "purpose" as a perplexing problem. The "purpose" of the poem, like the Eliotic "meat" of meaning, is what can be possessed and known by the reader only as that which is already "washed away by magnitude," dissolved and disseminated in an unstemmed sea of multiple forms and images. What is possessed, then, is an elliptical bottom of poetry that echoes with the polyphony of metaphor. What remains undissolved in the poem's verbal magnitude is the sign of a literal purpose that will not redeploy its own interference. This sign, which marks the perpetual deferral of an undissolvable poetic bottom as "the half they can never possess," can only be an ellipsis that designates such a purpose as a "still-starred" omission, as the end of a Peircean infinite regression of signs that, as both Eliot's dissertation and Stevens' "Notes" suggest, can have no end, for such an end term (the Peircean object) can be constituted only as the redeployment of the difference it was envisioned as closing. The canto suggests that this "purpose" is another elliptical site of difference and interference calling for another methodological interpretation. The serpent's poison and the disruptive boreal wind are "invincible," sweeping here through the figure of the poem as a re-presentational home for a central intentionality. But like Wishwood, which, as the expression of Amy's will to overpower difference, becomes the site of death, "the house will crumble and the books will burn" as the cataleptic, entropic hermeneutics of identity and poetic purpose encounter the differential energy of the auroras.

The fourth canto sums up the energetic disruption that blows through these earlier figures in the line, "The cancellations, / The negations are never final" (CP, 414). We must read this line in its most radical sense. Like homeless error in Eliot's dissertation or the curse written under everything in *The Family Reunion,* in "The Auroras" there is never a place, never a figure, never a methodological interpretation, never a bottom to poetry's labyrinthine sea of words that is not constituted as the site of negation and interference. All of poetry's central figures, like those Stevens mentions when he writes about the strictly methodological laws of modern physics, emerge differentially with a declination that cancels their ultimate significance. The "father" of the poem, in other words, must be thought of not as a substantial essence—an idea, concept, purpose, or meaning—represented in words but as the energetic interference repeated by every word. It is the father, in this canto, who speaks the truth— he says "no to no and yes to yes." However, he, like the Eumenides (whose presence disturbs strict categorical thinking), interferes with the ultimate justification of this truth and of both categorical assertion and denial by also saying yes to no. This father is the redeployment of endless cancellation and interference, and his "yes" marks Stevens' farewell to the illusion of a determinate cognitive core to poetry and his reenactment of a radically Nietzschean Will to Power. In Stevens, all yes's and no's are radically complementary "balances that happen" and must be thought without appeal to some ultimately justifying identity of truth.

There can be no name for this essential interference, for it cancels any figurative identity. It cannot be traced in poetry except as interference and noise, for while the "flights of eye and ear" discern the "supernatural preludes" that presumably announce the advent of the father, these discernments are nevertheless of "actors approaching, in company, in their masks." As the final question of the canto suggests, this redeployment of the theater of trope can only problematically "choir it with the naked wind" and only figuratively represent in a mask the boreal interferences moving through all companies of figures. The "master seated by the fire" is the constituting difference that cannot be accounted for in a name, is an additional *and yet*—"And yet in space and motionless and yet / Of motion the ever-brightening origin / / Profound and yet the king and yet the crown"—that disruptively intervenes in any throne, nest, room, or cabin, any architectural "maze / Of body and air and forms and images," any book or scene of writing.

The fifth canto's "festival" is a performance in the theater of trope that, characterized by its paraphernalia ("Scenes of the theatre, vistas and blocks of woods / And curtains like a naive pretense of sleep"), stages a drama of writing and representation (CP, 415). The company performs the "instinctive poem" (what "Notes" calls the "inflexible order"), a play of the father to whose voice, or "trumpet," the "unherded herds" of trope are obedient. In this sense, Canto V arises as an answer to the question that closes Canto IV, for it figures a representational company (a poem or nest or image) whose purpose is to "choir it [to substantialize in its dancing performance and to sing about in its song of words] with the naked wind," to represent the force of difference Canto IV describes as the father and origin of poetry's maze of representations. But as the earlier cantos suggest, because this fathering force cannot be represented except as a cancelling interference within representation itself, the festival of the father, the fated and "instinctive poem" of representation, must finally be a tragedy, the reenactment of the essential declination (for Eliot, the essential heterogeneity) of trope that marks its constituting difference from any master. All scenes in the theater of trope, all writings in the representational festival of whose tumult we always find ourselves a part, disclose the improvisational nature of their figures; each is part of the "disordered mooch" whose essential characteristic is that it has no essential core of significance, that "there are no lines to speak." Everything takes place in this representational festival as improvisational play, as the declination from any hermeneutical script. An origin always appears in this semiological world, for it performs the "instinctive poem" of the father. His figure, however, is a strategic improvisation whose appearance marks the eternal (and invigorating) return of interference and difference.

The poem's festival of the father, then, finally discloses itself as a "theatre floating through the clouds, / Itself a cloud," as a never-ending series of displacements in which improvised figures of substance—"of misted rock / And mountains running like water"—are translated into other such insubstantial figures (CP, 416).

It is of cloud transformed
To cloud transformed again, idly, the way
A season changes color to no end. (CP, 416)

The theater of trope is structurally identical to the Peircean infinite regression of signs, in which the irrelevant clothing of metaphor and figure is never exchanged for the neutrality of naked meaning but only for more signs. In Stevens, these transformations and exchanges are idle and come to no end, both in the sense that there is no point at which they stop—no final term to the transformations of trope—and in the sense that there is no transcendent purpose or profound significance to these improvisations. Crispin's verbal sea was always tossing up figures of its grounding shore, only to wash each bottom away in another irreducible polyphony of signification, and the representational festival of "The Auroras" traces in itself a similar difference. In its theater of trope there always appears "a capitol," the site of the law, but its authority is played out only along with the *clinamen* of interference; it "is emerging or has just / Collapsed." Neither present nor absent as such, this figure of representation's capitol, what "The Man with the Blue Guitar" terms "a bar in space. / / Sand heaped in the clouds," redeploys the differential relationship in which both law and declination emerge as copulars that are the differences they make to each other (CP, 179). For Stevens, the unending transformations of poetry's improvisational "half-thought of forms" suggest the differential essence of the theater of trope. Nietzsche notes the similarly improvisational characteristic of language when he writes that "the whole material [language] in which and with which the man of truth, the investigator, the philosopher works and builds, originates, if not from Nephelococcygia, cloudland, at any rate not from the essence of things."[8] Like Eliot's poetic meaning, the point of interference in which both meaty significance and rhetorical trick are essentially complicated, Stevens' clouds are both the central material and the immaterial improvisations of poetry.

The figural transformations of language's theater of trope thus lead to no final resolution, and the denouement, the untying of these transformations in the revelation of a central literality, "has to be postponed." The figure of the denouement suggests, as it did in

8. Friedrich Nietzsche, "Truth and Falsity in an Ultramoral Sense," in *The Philosophy of Nietzsche*, ed. Geoffrey Clive (New York, 1965), 507.

"The Comedian," the untying of a textual knot and the resolution of the text's complications in a unifying solution. In other words, the denouement brings to mind both the point at which the improvisations of the text stop and the secure bottom on which the reader can stand to survey (and master in his reading) the text's verboseness. But a Stevensian denouement is an unraveling of its own significance as a figure of textual resolution. In the idle drift of improvisation into improvisation, the "denouement has to be postponed," not because there is an ideal solution to the problem of the text that is simply absent or that cannot be made to appear, but because any textual denouement, any "capitol" or essential significance, ties up the text and resolves its loose ends only in another figure, another improvised solution, whose significance, like the haphazard denouement of "The Comedian" or Agatha's rune in *The Family Reunion,* unravels into a multitude of threads. The denouement, then, figures both a tying together and an unraveling of the text and thus discloses the interference that marks any denouement as an improvisation, as the redeployment of a problem and not as the simplicity of a solution. Even the assertion that "the denouement has to be postponed" unravels with the intervention of the succeeding stanza. This—the figure of language as a groundless cloudland of differentially constituted improvisations—

> This is nothing until in a single man contained,
> Nothing until this named thing nameless is
> And is destroyed. (CP, 416)

The figure of the theater of trope asserts a truth about language; it names literally, with certainty, and thus resolves the divagations of improvisation to an essential core of truth. This truth, however, does not escape the interference repeated by all assertions, all names, and all denouements. This "named thing," this name for the essence of language, is nothing until interrupted by its own cancellation, until it is nameless and destroyed. In this destructive cancellation and not in the assertion of a nameable essence is reenacted the interfering difference in which all names are constituted. It is the eternal return of this difference that frightens the "scholar of one candle" in the disclosure of an "Arctic effulgence," an auroral radiance irreducible to the identity of a cognitive sun.

It is also this difference that "leaps," like the father in Canto IV, through us and "all our heavens" as a canceling or extinguishing of such figures of transcendent significance, thus leaving,

> . . . of where we were and looked, of where
> We knew each other and of each other thought,
> A shivering residue, chilled and foregone,
> Except for that crown and mystical cabala. (CP, 417)

This interference, named here the "imagination," has, like error in Eliot's dissertation, no proper, determinate site (it is both "in snow" and "in the sky") and thus "takes its place" only as that which moves within any place as the cancellation of its significance. To name this force the "imagination" is therefore not to capture this endless cancellation in a representation or name but rather to trace in this name the interference or extinguishing that constitutes it. Like the name in Eliot's dissertation, which marks the interference of intended denotation by accident and chance improvisation, the name in Stevens is the trace or "shivering residue" of the interference that both constitutes it and cancels the identity of its significance (KE, 127). Its status as residual trace is the inevitable condition of representation and the name, just as, for Nietzsche, the foregone condition of our logic and our ideas is their appearance "only as the *residuum of a metaphor*," only as the traces of the irreducible metaphoricalness that cancels their literality.[9] "The imagination"—this canto's name for the difference that inhabits all names—must finally disclose itself as another improvisation in the theater of trope and not as tropes' mastering essence. It must "change from destiny to slight caprice," from the enthroned master figure to a haphazardly improvised denouement. There is for Stevens no name that is not its own "stele," the sign of its negation and the story of its "jetted tragedy," since its "mournful making" must inevitably "move to find / What must unmake it," just as (in "Notes") "two things of opposite nature seem to depend / On each other" and each is "in the other . . . included." The name here traces the complication of the serious with the capricious, of destiny with improvisation.

The interference reenacted by each scene in the theater of trope constructs the "tragic and desolate background" that Stevens sug-

9. *Ibid.*, 509.

gests, in a letter to Mona Von Duyn, the auroral lights symbolize. Against this background the poem's eighth canto plays out its meditations upon innocence as the idea of "pure principle": as the ideal ground uncontaminated by the improvisations of language's "mooch" (LWS, 852; CP, 418). Recalling the bodiless ideality of the first canto's serpent and the silent moment of Becket's decision in *Murder,* this innocence can be thought of only as a "still-starred" ideal that is neither of time nor of place. This ideal is appealed to (most often by Eliot the theologian) as a "sense against calamity," as a transcendence not subject to the poisoning improvisations of the "body" of representations in time and space.

But like all Stevensian figures of an uncontaminated purity at the bottom of language's poisonous verboseness, this pure ideality discloses the elliptical nature that is its end. A figure of the closure of improvisation in a pristine ideality, innocence, like Eliot's poetic meaning, can finally be thought only as a problematic site of difference, as the overlapping of desire and frustration. Its nature and its end constitutes the quintessential fact of the interference to which the ancient cycle of desire—the will to overpower difference—is the human response. Innocence is never innocently neutral; rather, like the Eumenides and the auroras, it insists upon the difference that constitutes it. The problem with the "pure principle," which in its ideality should function like a universal law transcending all local differences, is that it has only local, improvised significance—at some times it is "beautiful and true," while at others it is "beautiful but untrue." Thus

> It is like a thing of ether that exists
> Almost as predicate. But it exists,
> It exists, it is visible, it is, it is. (CP, 418)

Innocence names the insubstantial difference that constitutes all predication; it traces in the assertion *it is* the incommensurable significance, the improvised *almost* of metaphor and the *like* of analogy, that interferes with its neutral, innocent identity.

Thus when the canto arrives at its resolving denouement,

> So, then, these lights are not a spell of light,
> A saying out of a cloud, but innocence.
> An innocence of the earth and no false sign
> Or symbol of malice, (CP, 418)

and asserts the destined significance ("innocence") of the auroral lights, it does so only within the "idiom / Of the work," only through the mediations of the *as if* that mark this "drama that we live" as another haphazard performance in the theater of trope, another dream of innocence interrupted by the "guilty dream" of improvisation and trope. These mediations figure the "innocent mother" singing of the "innocent earth" and tell a story of a home untroubled by "the enigma of the guilty dream." This is the story of propriety and resolution in which the endlessly homeless and decentering auroral lights attain an immanent, univocal significance not interfered with by the possibility of its being another improvised "false sign." It is the story of a prelapsarian paradise before the differentiations of time that set brother against brother, the story, like Amy's of Wishwood, of the original brotherhood of man that is simultaneously the story of the originally univocal significance of words and signs. An Apollonian dream of just boundaries, here the "outlandish"—the figure of the alien and unaccountable—is banished beyond the borders of this homeland.

Although we "lay sticky with sleep," there is an "activity of fate" moving within this staged innocence—the interference that is the fate of representation and of the festival of figure and trope inside of whose noisy, tumultuous improvisations we inevitably find ourselves. It is the fate of the dream of an innocent, pure principle to disclose the additional significance—the "enigma of the guilty dream"—characteristic of its local idiom, an interference that disturbs and disrupts the dream with the question, "Shall we be found hanging in the trees next spring?" (CP, 419). This question traces an insistent difference, an incommensurability, or a "freedom of the two" that cannot be reduced to a univocal solution, for it is at once a figure of innocence (of the rebirth and growth of ourselves as springtime fruit) and a figure of guilt (of a death by hanging). This plurality of significance suggests an "imminence" that cancels the dream of innocence, for any answer must be a difference-collapsing interpretation, a local improvisation, or a practical solution with no ultimate justification. Imminent as an "activity of fate" in the apparent simplicity of innocence is the force of disaster that doubles innocence as a sign of guilt and that intervenes in the pure "innocence of the earth" with the improvisations of the "false sign." This disaster repeats the poison of Canto I and draws attention to what

The Family Reunion calls the "curse" written on the underside of everything—the irreducible possibility that no transcendent principle is pure and simple, that all truths are local improvisations of trope, incommensurable images "at the end of the cave." This unforgettable disaster interferes with the sun as the metaphor of ideal, transcendent truth, disrupting its privileged status and returning it to a field of multiple suns with no central core, to a field in which the sun shines only with a local significance. It is the disaster redeployed by the figure of the auroras, of local, improvised principles or truths without a reconciling center. Like the difference that Eliot affirms in his dissertation as "essential" but later seeks to obscure in his appeals to a core of sacramental truth, difference in Stevens may be "the tenderest and the truest part" of innocence; it is the lack of a script, the deficiency in the theater of trope, that constitutes its improvisational freedom. With Stevens, "We stand in the tumult of a festival" of linguistic and epistemological improvisations, and there is no place to stand, no privileged observation point, that is not already one of the festival's eccentric vistas.

"The Auroras of Autumn" ends on an improvisation no less problematic than the serpent figure that opened it, or the rune at the end of *The Family Reunion*, or the barbering at the end of "The Comedian." This figure, in the poem's tenth canto, is that of the "never-fading genius" who, like the serpent figure contrived to make us "sure of sun," tropes the closure of his meditations upon a "whole, / The full of fortune and the full of fate" (CP, 420). Hidden within the "secretive syllables" read to the congregation is this figure of the secret essence, the vital and fulfilling genius, the bodiless "spectre of the spheres," hidden at their center. The text the rabbi is to read is the sacramental story of innocent re-presentation, of a language whose genius, whose cognitive core, is fulfilled and expressed by its different meditations. But this story of representation is so overlaid with mediations and qualifications that it becomes, finally, a polyphony of different significances and an indelibly contaminated article of hermeneutical faith. The canto begins by tracing the possibilities implicit in the differential relationships of people to the world, possibilities that, in their playfully changing phases, recall the inconstancy of the moon's ever-changing light. It then turns "back to where we were when we began," choosing to solemnize and mark as a nota the proposition, "An unhappy people in a happy world." But this return discloses the haphazard improvisa-

tion of the choice and the strictly methodological nature of this reduced and simple beginning.

This improvised beginning—like the pretense, as Eliot suggests
in the dissertation, on which we build our theories—sets the stage
for the "contrivance of the spectre of the spheres," the genius
whose meditations appear to close on something other than another improvisation (KE, 167). But such a genius can be staged only
within the textual space opened by the improvised beginning and
thus appears as another rhetorical contrivance. Because this interference is the constituting condition of such an ideal essence, "the
cancellings, / The negations"—the improvisational nature of any
such cognitive core that interferes with its identification as an essential genius—"are never final." What the solemnized, "secretive syllables" of poetry seem to hide under the guise of metaphor and figure is a "never-failing genius," a profound identity and significance.
The unfilterable interference, however, suggests that poetry may always be simply pretending to be such a disguise, hiding instead another local improvisation. This is the additional possibility, the echo
or extra mark, that interrupts any unraveling of the textual knot,
any secure wading through poetry's sea of words, any denouement
to the improvisations of the theater of trope. "The Auroras of Autumn" ends in a deferral of knowledge (what is it that the genius
might know?), in a haphazard denouement lit not by the punctual
illumination of a transcendent center of truth but by the immaterial
improvisations, the ever-changing patterns constituted as the differential interferences of energies and forces, figured by the auroral
lights.

Five
Dancing to *Four Quartets*

The interferences that energize much of Eliot's writing—the inter-ruptions of Eliot the theologian by Eliot the semiologist—appear again in the two interpretations of history that resonate in the third section of "Little Gidding": "History may be servitude, / History may be freedom" (CPP, 142). Eliot continued these reflections on history eight years after the publication of *Four Quartets* in his introduction to the Cresset Press edition of *The Adventures of Huckleberry Finn*. The introduction, which reads the novel's major figures (Huck, Tom, and the river), also reads retrospectively the similar figures of the river, the bridge, and the Word that are preva-lent in the earlier poem. In isolating the narrative force that makes Twain's book a masterpiece, Eliot's introductory remarks focus upon the powerful rhythms of the River and the tensive energy re-leased both by those rhythms and by the interaction of Huck and Tom. For Eliot, *Tom Sawyer* and *The Adventures of Huckleberry Finn* are distinctly different books, and the appearance of Huck and the river in the later book clearly articulates this difference. His reading of these figures traces an interpretation of history and its book that marks in both a certain uncontrollable freedom, an ex-cess of energy and peregrination (akin to the wandering of the Monchensey history) that cannot be explained by the alternative in-terpretation that understands history, or the book in which it is

written, as servitude. The difference between freedom and servitude, between an open-ended book resistant to a hermeneutical
law and a book defined as the incarnation of that law, is central to
Eliot's reading of Twain's novel and to his earlier reading of history's
texture in *Four Quartets*.

It is the river, for Eliot, that gives *Huckleberry Finn* its form, sav-
ing it from the servile determinism of sequentiality. "A sequence of
adventures with a happy ending" would be a closed form bounded
by determinable beginning and end points whose differences are
spanned by the sequential logic of cause and effect. The dominant
purveyor of such a closed narrative is Tom himself, whom Eliot describes as a "lively boy who has read a good deal of romantic fiction" (HF, xii, viii). Tom's romanticism is apparent in the various
dramas he directs in both the beginning and ending sections of
Huckleberry Finn, dramas that intrude on the novel as restagings of
previous narrative fictions.

> "Ransomed? What's that?"
> "I don't know. But that's what they do. I've seen it in books; and so of
> course that's what we've got to do." (HF, 9)

For Tom, the authority of romantic fictions is unshakably sacred,
and his dramatic stagings reflect that belief. "It don't make no difference how foolish it is, it's the *right* way—and it's the regular
way. And there ain't no *other* way, that ever *I* heard of, and I've
read all the books that gives any information about these things."
The "right way" to stage or structure an event, the way of the romantic fiction, is for Tom to invent a sequence of actions that repeats precisely and is circumscribed completely by his sacred texts.
Each event is intended to be a story with a determinable beginning
and a happy ending. Each event is, therefore, a staging of a romance
that understands history as *Heilsgeschichte* (the way Eliot himself
sought to interpret history in *Murder*), as a career in which differences begin in a punctual site and end in a similar unity (HF, 244,
xvi). Tom's stagings repeat this logic of history as servitude to an
organizing underpattern of identity.

But according to Eliot, *Huckleberry Finn* is not one of Tom's romantic dramas, for its form is not that of the closed book but that of
a "very big and powerful river." Such a river "can wholly determine
the course of human peregrination." Eliot repeatedly emphasizes
this illimitable quality of the River, its unrestrictable force and en-

ergy. The river, like the "Dionysiac flood tide" Nietzsche describes as periodically destroying "all the little circles in which the Apollonian would confine Hellenism," appears as that which can treacherously and capriciously exceed its own boundaries and inundate the land that only provisionally defines its margins. Eliot succinctly traces the natural force of the river when he observes that it "is never wholly chartable; it changes its pace, it shifts its channel, unaccountably: it may suddenly efface a sandbar, and throw up another where before was navigable water." In her discussion of the relationship between Eliot's introduction and "The Dry Salvages," Lois Cuddy assumes that the river is unchartable because "of what is hidden beneath its surface or what is waiting ahead," but this interpretation evades what is most radical in Eliot's figure. There is no writing, no chart or map, adequate to the river, not because it hides something under its surface, but because it is a dynamic system constituted by change and accident. Disrupting any boundary that would enclose it, the River "cannot tolerate any design," and thus it is the declination, the interference, that inhabits any pattern or account of it (HF, xii, xiii, xvi). It is homeorrhetic and can be thought of, within what Michel Serres has called the "thermodynamics of open systems," as "a river that flows and yet remains stable in the continual collapse of its banks and the irreversible erosion of the mountains around it." [1] As Eliot employs it, the river tropes an energy at the center of *Huckleberry Finn*, an energy that can best be characterized as a continual redeployment of difference. For Eliot, it is the differential energy that he traces in the metaphor of the river that makes Twain's book "a great book" (HF, xv).

Like the river, whose beginning ("In the beginning, it is not yet the River") and whose end ("in its end, it is no longer the River") are only practical improvisations, the book begins and ends with accounts of Tom's staged romances, disclosing the contrivance that supplies the text with the fictions of its own beginning and end,

---

1. Friedrich Nietzsche, "*The Birth of Tragedy*" and "*The Genealogy of Morals*," trans. Francis Golffing (New York, 1956), 65; Lois A. Cuddy, "Eliot and *Huck Finn*: River and Sea in 'The Dry Salvages,'" *T. S. Eliot Review*, III (1976), 8; Michel Serres, *Hermes: Literature, Science, Philosophy*, ed. Josuè V. Harari and David F. Bell (Baltimore, 1982), 74. An editors' note defines homeorrhesis: "The word 'homeorrhesis' is formed from the Greek words *homos*, meaning 'same,' and *rhysis*, meaning 'flow.' Serres replaces the normal term describing the equilibrium of a self-regulating system, 'homeostasis,' by 'homeorrhesis' in order to emphasize the idea of continual movement and exchange as opposed to the less dynamic idea of stasis."

with, that is, the romantic fiction of the closed account. The river is bounded by its multiple headwaters and its disseminating delta, just as the narration is bounded by its beginning and its ending, but in both cases these boundaries are the sites of irreducible difference. Huck, who, like the river, "has no beginning and no end," can only disappear in order to make room for the stage manager who brings the text to its improvised close "in a cloud of whimsicalities" (HF, xvi). For Eliot, such closure of the differential energy figured by both Huck and the river emerges only as a methodological contrivance that, like the beginnings and endings of many of Stevens' poems, obscures difference in its romantically orchestrated performance.

Thus Eliot discovers an underlying tension in *Huckleberry Finn*, a tension that traces two interpretations of the significance of the concept "book." One interpretation, reflected by Tom's dramatic stagings, romantically views books and the history they represent as closed forms bounded by fixed beginnings and ends and overseen by the logic of sequentiality that leads them to their happy endings. This static figure, however, is eroded by what Eliot finds to be most significant about *Huckleberry Finn:* the fact that it is not a book in this romantic sense. This interpretation stresses the differential energy that flows within the writing, an energetic heterogeneity that, by exceeding and differing from any hermeneutical pattern or cognitive boundary, repeats as parody the closure of the romantic "book." In Eliot's introduction, Twain's book does not take the form of a bridge that, by joining its beginning to its end, spans with a reconciling identity the differences within its writing. Rather, taking its form from the river, it appears as a limitless field of differences that cannot be finally bridged by any structure—a meaning or concept, for example—that seeks its closure and containment. Since the origin and end of this written river emerge only as improvisations within the stream itself, such conceptual bridges (like the logic of sequentiality) are never other than methodological stagings, incidental dramas that, like Stevens' "balances that happen," only figuratively mark writing's beginning and end. The river of the text, the differential energy of writing, breaks all such conceptual bridges, what Nietzsche calls the "rainbow-bridges of concepts" that, like words and sounds, are "rainbows and illusive bridges between things which are eternally apart," intervening in the romantic "book" and disturbing its stability. The river of writing is fluid, dynamic, and living, writes Serres: "What is slowly destroyed is the solid basin. The fluid is stable; the solid which wears away is unstable—Heraclitus and Parmenides were both right. Hence the notion of homeorrhesis. The living system is homeorrhetic."[2] Like Stevens' theater of trope it flows from one metaphorical improvisation to another, redeploying the difference that separates staged beginning from staged ending. We have seen this dynamic differential energy before in Eliot; the Eumenides marked its deployment in *The Family Reunion*. But in that play it was still somewhat obscured by Eliot's earlier will to overpower difference. As we noted earlier, however, *The Family Reunion* suggests an alteration in Eliot's thinking about difference—from life's curse to its dynamic energy—that results in the affirmation of the *Huckleberry Finn* introduction. Here, Eliot the theologian, in whose earlier will to power difference was obscured, can be seen as one of Zarathustra's "blockheads," believing that "Whatever is *over* the river is firm; all the values of things, the bridges, the concepts . . . all that is *firm*."[3]

In his comments upon Eliot's "literature of waste," Richard Poirier observes that the poet's "genius is most impressive when his language challenges the conceptual and poetic schemas on which he seems to depend."[4] Such a challenge is apparent in the *Huckleberry Finn* introduction, which repeats the enterprise of all introductory remarks: to stand outside the text as an observer-elect to provide commentary upon or interpretation of it for the reader before he begins his own reading. Introductions conventionally supply the reader with a map for his passage through the text, a pattern of ideas, images, or characters that can guide him through the river of writing into which he seeks to plunge. An introduction appears as a sign of the critic's will to have power over his subject, which he stages as a solved problem spanned by his overseeing glance. The words of the critic describe and explain the words of the text, and thus the pretext of the introduction is the same as that reflected by Tom's dramas: the romantic fiction of closure, of a narration bounded by a beginning and an end. Eliot's introduction to *Huckleberry Finn*, however, interferes with the "poetic schema" upon

2. Friedrich Nietzsche, *The Will to Power*, trans. Walter Kaufmann and R. J. Hollingdale (New York, 1967), 225; and *Thus Spoke Zarathustra*, trans. Walter Kaufmann (New York, 1954), 217; Serres, *Hermes*, 74.

3. Nietzsche, *Zarathustra*, 201.

4. Richard Poirier, *The Performing Self* (New York, 1971), 48.

which introductions rely—the schema of the closed book and the bridging concept. Since *Huckleberry Finn* is not a book with a happy ending but an unchartable river of differential energy—a form that parodies form—its introduction emerges as a critique of introductions, a parody of itself, a commentary on *Huckleberry Finn* suggesting that there can be no observer-elect and, therefore, that all commentaries are romantic improvisations.

Four Quartets is a similarly doubled commentary upon history, books, and words. When "Little Gidding" juxtaposes history as servitude and as freedom, it foreshadows the dynamic tension Eliot later traces in *Huckleberry Finn* between the servile fiction of the closed book and the freedom of writing's differential energy. This tension deploys the difference from which *Four Quartets* emerges, and it is within this difference—in the margins between the lines of these two interpretations—that the poem is written. Where history is understood as servitude, it recounts the romantic story of the containment of the differential energy of words, the spanning of the river of writing with a "rainbow-bridge" that renders its figures redeemable for a core of literal meaning, a beginning or ending of difference in the revelation of truth. But where history is understood as freedom, it is always another story. The bridge shows itself not as a gesture of closure, but as an illimitable process of transfiguration, as a peregrination that, like a Peircean infinite chain of signs, carries figure into figure and repeatedly renews, "in another pattern," the liberating, energetic dance of difference that is the form of the river of writing. We recall that for Stevens, too, "poetry constantly requires a new relation" (CPP, 142; OP, 178).

The bridge, then, tropes incommensurable hermeneutic stances vis-à-vis writing, stances that interfere with each other most dramatically in the first section of "The Dry Salvages," the portion of *Four Quartets* for which the *Huckleberry Finn* introduction appears almost as a retrospective gloss. As in that later preface, the river here figures a force or energy—a musical rhythm—that is finally uncontainable (CPP, 130). "Sullen, untamed and intractable," this energetic rhythm is reflected again by the pulse of the sea's waves which bring to land the "hints of earlier and other creation," the breakage of "losses" that erodes the security of any creation, any machine or artifact (sieve, lobsterpot, oar, or gear) constructed in man's will to have power over the energy of the sea. It is finally described as the "ground swell," a pulsatory force that "is and was from the beginning" and that, as the river "within us" and the sea "all about us," is no ground for human endeavor but is rather a swelling rhythm, a field of force or differential, pulsatory energy in which human endeavor is constructed and plays itself out.

When Nietzsche writes in *The Twilight of the Idols* of that "wonderful phenomenon which bears the name Dionysus," he notes that it is explicable only as an "overflowing . . . *excess* of energy"—only, that is, as a declination from any explanation. The river of "The Dry Salvages" and the differential, pulsatory energy it figures suggest a similar declination, a "reminder / Of what men choose to forget." Its interfering excess can only be figuratively accounted for, charted, or spanned by "the builder of bridges" and by the "dwellers in cities" for whom the river is "almost forgotten." Bridging—the constructing of a machine or artifact to span the "intractable" and obliterate the "frontier"—*almost* makes its builder forget that it emerges out of and is reliant upon the difference of which its very existence is a sign. Here in "The Dry Salvages," the noise that accompanies the contrivance of a difference-collapsing cognitive core, muted earlier by Eliot's sacramental hermeneutics but broadcast by Stevens' delicately clinking improvisations, is played loudly. As John Carlos Rowe remarks about that most famous of American bridges (Hart Crane's), "to 'bridge' is always to declare the emptiness of the pure act and its dependence upon the abyss to be spanned."[5] The interference—the difference that is the abyss—remains. Unchartable and intractable, it is an excess that reminds the "worshippers of the machine" of the artifice of what Nietzsche calls the "firm."

Such worshipers, like the "anxious worried women" who appear at the end of this first section, are, like Eliot himself in *Murder in the Cathedral,* readers of time, critics or interpreters whose project is to "unweave, unwind, unravel / And piece together the past and future" into a continuous history, into a formal, unified closure of a complete book (CPP, 131). Their time, like the chronologies of "Notes" and the servile sequentiality that *Huckleberry Finn* rejects, is defined by chronometers, machines that pattern past, present, and future into the circular movement of hands about a clockface. For these women, history is a text to be read and unraveled, an oceanic speech to be spanned by a unifying thread of explanation. But the

5. Friedrich Nietzsche, *"Twilight of the Idols" and "The Anti-Christ,"* trans. R. J. Hollingdale (New York, 1968), 108; John Carlos Rowe, "The 'Super-Historical' Sense of Hart Crane's *The Bridge*," *Genre*, XI (Winter, 1978), 598.

sea's ground swell "measures time not our time . . . a time / Older than chronometers." Chronometric time renders history as servile to the firmness of the sequencing machine, to the logic of cause and effect, but the differential pulse that energizes the first section of "The Dry Salvages" remains as a reminder of the artifice of such rendering.

If we follow the drifting wreckage of the artificially firm back toward the beginning of *Four Quartets*, we arrive at the second section of "Burnt Norton," in which the "drift of stars" reconciles the "dance along the artery" (which looks forward to the later pulse of waves) and the "circulation of the lymph" into a pattern that, like a constellation of stars, is itself continually drifting and dispersing and is therefore a parodic figure of the infirmity of reconciling patterns (CPP, 118, 119). This section of *Four Quartets* is itself patterned, as Finn Bille has pointed out, by a particular style of rhetoric, which he describes as the "choreography" of the "limbo-image." Bille defines such an image as a metaphor that "negates both its terms, negates a comparison on the literal level, and leaves the mind to explore the limbo between the two negations."[6] Profoundly anti-Hegelian, what is important about the limbo-image is the space between the two negated words, the margin disclosed as a difference that, because of the mutual negation of the differing words, cannot be spanned by a third, reconciling word. The limbo-image thus names the propulsive force of a certain rhetoric, and it is this dancing force that energizes *Four Quartets*. In "Burnt Norton II" this rhetoric finds its greatest concentration: "Neither flesh nor fleshless; / Neither from nor towards"; "neither arrest nor movement"; "Neither movement from nor movement towards, / Neither ascent nor decline" (CPP, 119).

It is within this highly concentrated rhetoric that the figure of the "still point" first emerges in *Four Quartets*, appearing as the point upon which the dance of the world turns. The dance arises out of this point ("Except for the point, the still point, / There would be no dance"), but the point is itself a dancing participant, for "there is only the dance." The still point emerges only as a site of difference deployed within the differential rhetoric of the limbo-image. Like the river, it marks an unbridgeable difference, a tensive differentia-

---

6. Finn Bille, "The Ultimate Metaphor and the Defeat of Poetry in T. S. Eliot's *Four Quartets*," *International Journal of Symbology*, III (March, 1972), 17.

tion that continually constitutes the dance. It redeploys the differential energy that propels the turning world of dancing rhetoric, the difference without which there would be no dance and, therefore, nothing.

A sign of the world's irresolvable openness and therefore also of the openness of rhetoric and language, the still point is a parodic metaphor that, like the sun in many of Stevens' poems, interferes with and sets dancing the static fixity it appears to name. It is in this sense similar to Crane's "primordial One," which, as Rowe observes, is the "energy of differences" and "never a synthesis that would destroy those tensive and productive relations." The manifestation of these tensive relations is, for Eliot, the dance itself, a liberating dance of differential freedom without a fixing pattern that, like the capricious, excessive flooding of the river in *Huckleberry Finn,* can never be defined by a hermeneutical law or a determining choreography. Viewed from this perspective, Eliot's dance recalls that of Nietzsche, who asserts, through Zarathustra, "I would believe only in a god who could dance." Zarathustra's animals describe a turning world opened not by a transcendent deity but by the eternal recurrence of the differential dance: "To those who think as we do, all things themselves are dancing. . . . In every Now, being begins; round every Here rolls the sphere There. The center is everywhere. Bent is the path of eternity." This world dances not to the choreography of a fixed pattern but, like Stevens' incidental balances, "on the feet of chance," its site being the "dance floor for divine accidents." In *The Twilight of the Idols,* this dancing becomes a characteristic of writing itself. "For *dancing* in any form cannot be divorced from a *noble education,* being able to dance with the feet, with concepts, with words: do I still have to say that one has to be able to dance with the pen—that *writing* has to be learned?" And in *The Gay Science* dancing shows itself to be the sign of a good philosopher. "I would not know what the spirit of a philosopher might wish more to be than a good dancer." Michel Haar reads Nietzsche's dancing style of writing as having the aim of "destroying, or at least checkmating, all logical and, especially, dialectical 'seriousness,' the goal of which is always to establish identities or to reveal the one absolute Identity."[7] This casual, flippant

7. Rowe, "The 'Super-Historical' in Crane," 611; Nietzsche, *Zarathustra,* 41, 217–18, 166, "*Twilight of the Idols,*" 66, and *The Gay Science,* trans. Walter Kauf-

checkmating can readily be seen in Stevens' poems, but it is also the effect of Eliot's figures of the river and the still point, which both suggest and interfere with a logical commentary or dialectical choreography. These figures reflect the differential energy of Eliot's writing, the interference of the serious and the flippant, of identity and difference, that is a peculiarly Nietzschean "dance with the pen."

This dancing writing thus differentiates itself from any logical or dialectical structure of meaning that seeks to master its differential energy, to enclose it, for example, between the covers of a history that would mark its beginning in a determining cause and its ending in a determinate effect. Its place, in other words, is that of perpetual disaffection, a site "Burnt Norton III" describes as the "here" of the poem and Stevens characterizes as the perpetual exile of our images. This site is denoted, again, by the tension of the limbo-image: "Neither daylight . . . Nor darkness . . . Neither plenitude nor vacancy" (CPP, 120). A place of neither presence and revelation ("Investing form with lucid stillness") nor absence and concealment ("Emptying the sensual with deprivation"), it is lighted by a flicker, an interference of daylight and darkness that checkmates its identity with either one. Like the speech of the "god whose oracle is at Delphi" (*Four Quartets* often cites Heraclitus), the disaffected, dancing poem "neither speaks plainly nor conceals, but indicates by signs" that differentiate themselves from any improvised pretense of determination and meaning. The signs leave the "time-ridden faces"— those readers who, like the "anxious worried women" of "The Dry Salvages I" or the wading reader in Stevens, desire the mastery of the dance and the closure of difference—"Distracted from distraction by distraction / Filled with fancies and empty of meaning," chasing the traces of one distracting fancy, one Apollonian illusion, after another.[8] The world of these readers moves "In appetency, on its metalled ways / Of time past and time future," in the ancient cycle of a desire for the firm support of the bridging concept, the "metalled" span that could close the abysmal frontier. Their world's

---

mann (New York, 1974), 346; Michel Haar, "Nietzsche and Metaphysical Language," in David B. Allison (ed.), *The New Nietzsche: Contemporary Styles of Interpretation* (New York, 1977), 6–7.

8. Heraclitus of Ephesus, *On Nature*, trans. G. T. W. Patrick (Baltimore, 1888), 86, fragment XI.

metalled ways are described by property, sense, fancy, and spirit, those choreographed ideas interfered with by the differential flicker of writing's dance.

The "drift of stars" in "Burnt Norton II" is similarly reflected by a drift of words in "Burnt Norton V," which, recalling the figure of the dance itself, interrupts the entropic influence that their patterning into a grammar, poem, or book always exerts. Although "words move," a stillness is invoked by "the form, the pattern," a cessation of motion that is nevertheless only a pretense of stillness, since even a "Chinese jar still / Moves perpetually in its stillness." Similarly, the "stillness of the violin" and its note is an ever-moving stillness, a dynamic, homeorrhetic system, that lasts only while the energetic dance of air molecules continues. The stillness of the Chinese jar and of the violin are both patterns whose "detail . . . is movement," and thus it is only in the long view—in the fabricated hallucination of "Burnt Norton I" or the vision seen while "drowsing in sunlight" of the Marston essay—that stillness appears (CPP, 121, 122; EE, 194).

The form of words and music, however, is as alive with differential energy as is *Huckleberry Finn*'s river, for

> . . . Words strain,
> Crack and sometimes break, under the burden,
> Under the tension, slip, slide, perish,
> Decay with imprecision, will not stay in place,
> Will not stay still. (CPP, 121)

The slippage of words is apparent in the lines immediately preceding those quoted above, which, in an ostensible attempt to describe stillness, crackle with a dissonant tension marked by the mediations of the *not that only* and the *or say*, phrases like Stevens' *as if*'s and *and yet*'s that interfere with the cataleptic stillness of identity. Tension, drift, slippage, and energy describe words' continual movement as a field of force in which stillness appears not as a cessation of movement, not as a cognitive core beyond or beneath words' torrential, differential motion, but as part of their dance. The still point, the pattern, and the Word emerge out of and within the dance of words as sites of difference redeploying an energy that, like Heraclitus' river, "disperses and gathers again, or rather not again nor a second time, but at the same time it forms and is dissolved, it comes and goes." The "funeral dance" that attacks the "absolute

Identity" of the Word is only the differential complement of the dance in which it emerges.[9]

The hermeneutical stance that views history as servitude is thus a particular style of reading that, in its desire for stillness and closure, blinds itself to the differential energy of the signs it seeks to interpret. It reflects the sacramental hermeneutics deployed by Eliot in *Murder in the Cathedral, The Waste Land,* and *The Family Reunion* and by the rabbi in Stevens' "Notes," who sees in different figures the identity of "only one." This is the style recounted by the opening lines of "The Dry Salvages V" and marked by an understanding of signs as Peircean symbols, as representations of a transcendent identity:

> To communicate with Mars, converse with spirits,
> To report the behaviour of the sea monster,
> Describe the horoscope, haruspicate or scry,
> Observe disease in signatures, evoke
> Biography from the wrinkles of the palm
> And tragedy from fingers; release omens
> By sortelege, or tea leaves, riddle the inevitable
> With playing cards, fiddle with pentagrams
> Or barbituric acids, or dissect
> The recurrent image into pre-conscious terrors—
> To explore the womb, or tomb, or dreams; all these are usual
> Pastimes and drugs, and features of the press. (CPP, 135–36)

This list represents "Men's curiosity" that, like the anxiety of "worried women" in the first section, "searches past and future" for the firmness of an organizing truth beneath the destabilizing differences of time and its signs. Such a search attempts to read history once and for all as the representation of *Heilsgeschichte* that will reveal itself when history's signs are properly interpreted. This style of reading is structurally identical to the "occupation for the saint," whose interpretation of the "point of intersection of the timeless / With time," whose vision of reconciling stillness, comes, however, through a "lifetime's death in love" and not through "Pastimes and drugs, and features of the press." Both the sanctity of the saint and the anxiety of men, then, reflect a human wish to read in the signs of time a core of meaning. They manifest a will to overpower difference.

9. *Ibid.,* 94, note to fragment XLI; Haar, "Nietzsche and Metaphysical Language," 7.

Such a mystical apprehension is not, however, the occupation of the poet in *Four Quartets,* for whom there is no visionary identity but "only the unattended / Moment, the moment in and out of time" that Eliot describes as a "distraction fit." This moment recalls the endless detours of the "time-ridden faces" of "Burnt Norton III," who, in a quest for meaning, slide laterally from one fanciful distraction to another. Here in "The Dry Salvages V," however, their perpetual circulation, like the celestial ennui of apartments in Stevens, is seen not as a vicious circle of frustrated desire but as an affirmation of the differential energy whose figure is incarnation, the "moment in and out of time" that deploys the interference that is the being of all things. The distraction of the unattended moment leads to an energetic dance of "hints and guesses" that point not to a reconciling core of truth but only to more "Hints followed by guesses," to a transfigurative dance of improvisation and conjecture. These hints and guesses, then, are constituted differentially in a cognitive field without a central core. Because of this productive deficiency—because the field has no resolving solution—incarnation emerges as "the impossible union," as the aim that, since it is "Never here to be realised," affirms difference as essential. The repetition of this dancing difference is the "right action" of most of us, for it is in the trying—in the repetition of the aim whose realization is impossible and, therefore, of the difference that opens the transfigurative dance of "hints and guesses"—that we "are only undefeated." The trying, the will to overpower difference, redeploys the differential life of the dance that is itself the energetic dance of life, nourishing the "life of significant soil," out of which emerge other "hints and guesses," other texts and poems, which themselves continue the lateral sliding of an interminably open cognitive field.

This way of open-ended trying perpetually repeats the differential energy that forces open the enclosing hermeneutics of the "metalled ways / Of time past and time future," breaking apart their "firm" readings as readily as Nietzsche says that ice *breaks bridges.*[10] It is a way affirmed by the repetitions of "East Coker III," the section of *Four Quartets* that meditates upon the differential darkness marked by waiting. This fecund "darkness of God" is the vacant but tension-packed abyss between stars, the marginal *entr'acte* between two stagings in a theater, or the inexplicable interruption in the other-

10. Nietzsche, *Zarathustra,* 201.

wise chartable journey of the underground train from one stop to another. It discloses the existence of the between, of spacing, of the *nothing* of difference in which "the bold imposing façade" of the human architecture of ideas emerges only as a prop that is finally rolled away to make room for still another figurative façade. As in Stevens, the exchange is only of "theatre for theatre" and not of improvised performance for unimproved truth, or of a Peircean sign for a real object (CPP, 121, 127; CP, 309). Waiting in this darkness of difference is a "wait without hope" and "without love," a suspension of all causes and effects, beginnings and endings, an open-ended, tensive time of disaffection and difference. Even faith finds its origin in the temporal deferral troped by the wait, which, in its taking leave of "every wish for certainty," becomes a sign of radical, Nietzschean freedom, of a "dancing . . . near abysses."[11] The repetitive ending of this section marks within all certainties of knowledge, possession, and being an abysmal difference that energizes their entropic stillness into dancing, for

> In order to arrive at what you do not know
>   You must go by the way of ignorance.
> In order to possess what you do not possess
>   You must go by the way of dispossession.
> In order to arrive at what you are not
>   You must go through the way in which you are not. (CPP, 127)

This is the way of waiting, of the suspension of certainties (like Stevens' "difficultest rigor") by the perpetual disclosure of difference within the firm identities of knowledge, possession, and being. It is a way of radical freedom different from the "metalled ways" of hermeneutical servitude. It draws attention to the differential relationships in which knowledge and ignorance, possession and dispossession, presence and absence—all radically incommensurable ideas—emerge only as the differences they make to each other. This waiting is the dynamic, energetic way of the dance.

And it is the way of poetry and particularly of the poet who, in "East Coker V," writes

> So here I am, in the middle way, having had twenty years—
> Twenty years largely wasted, the years of *l'entre deux guerres*—
> Trying to learn to use words, and every attempt

11. Nietzsche, *Gay Science*, 289–90.

Is a wholly new start, a different kind of failure
Because one has only learnt to get the better of words
For the thing one no longer has to say, or the way in which
One is no longer disposed to say it. (CPP, 128)

Each beginning in this enterprise redeploys the essential heterogeneity of words. Each attempt repeats the differential energy that
opens writing not as the re-presentation of transcendent identity
but as a lateral sliding between failures, as another beginning in pretense or improvisation, and thus as the eternal return of a radically
Nietzschean Will to Power in which the differential characteristic of
all beginnings is affirmed.

Such a redeployment of difference is the "Home" from which
one starts, a home characterized as the pattern that is neither simply "the intense moment / Isolated, with no before and after" nor
simply "the lifetime of one man only" but rather a perplexing pattern of interferences, a "lifetime burning in every moment . . . of old
stones that cannot be deciphered." This home—the headwaters of
the river of writing—is thus a disclosure of writing's actual homelessness, of its constituting exile, since one starts only from other
texts ("old stones") that are themselves provocatively unreadable.
"East Coker" places the reader "close to the first—undecipherable—stone." There is, in other words, no home, no pure origin, no
beginning from which writing starts, nothing before the differential
dance of the "old stones that cannot be deciphered," no prefatory
pretext for poetry "that is not already a text." [12] "Old men ought to
be explorers," Eliot writes, in an exploration that is always a "still
moving" voyage, a lateral drift, through the vast waters of an interreferential sea of undecipherable texts without a noncontradictory
identity or a decipherable core of literal truth. It is a voyage in the
differential ebb and flow of a primordially disaffected and energetically disaffecting writing.

Four Quartets turns out to be an interminable adventure in an illimitable field of essentially heterogeneous signs, a voyage whose
source and destination are only improvisations that themselves
emerge as marks of the voyage's continuation. It is, in fact, the idea
of a literal destination for such a voyage, or the end of a Peircean

12. Jacques Derrida, *Dissemination*, trans. Barbara Johnson (Chicago, 1981),
358, 328.

infinite regression of signs, that "The Dry Salvages III," with its citation of the *Bhagavad-Gita,* calls into question. The passage revolves
around two figures of voyaging: the train, from which the "narrow-
ing rails slide together behind you," and the "drumming liner,"
whose wake "widens behind you" (CPP, 134). Both of these figures
are of mechanized bridges that obliterate spatial and temporal difference. The voyage figured by these bridges is thus a directed one
that spans the space between a fixed point of departure and a terminus. But such an understanding of voyaging, which is the sacramental understanding of history as servitude to a controlling pattern, or
a universal law of cause and effect, is challenged by Eliot's citation
of the Krishna speech directed toward "you who think you are voyaging." For Krishna, voyaging is not a determined movement between
a beginning and an end, but like the disaffected *here* of the poem, it
is rather a continual state of difference "between the hither and the
farther shore." Thus the passage cautions, "do not think of the fruit
of action. / Fare forward," since to tie the voyaging action to the
determination of a shore or a result is to desire a servile closure in
which the energetic freedom of the voyage is overlooked. Indeed, it
is the very understanding of fructification as closure that the passage disturbs, for although the "sphere of being" upon which the
"mind of man may be intent / At the time of death" appears as the
"one action . . . Which shall fructify in the lives of others," the fruit
can only repeat the death of its single, determinate source, since "the
moment of death is every moment." Moments are essentially multiple and differential, and it is the voyaging between them that redeploys the differences on which time depends. The differential *here*
of the poetic voyage is, according to Krishna, "your real destination"—a faring forward that has no destination, that is not a closed
journey between beginning and end but an interminable voyage of
seamen in the "here between."

When "East Coker II" renounces "the knowledge derived from
experience," it affirms the seminal voyaging of poetry, particularly of
Four Quartets (CPP, 125). The section opens with a romance of representational order, a cosmology in which

> Thunder rolled by the rolling stars
> Simulates triumphal cars
> Deployed in constellated wars
> Scorpion fights against the Sun
> Until the Sun and Moon go down

Comets weep and Leonids fly
Hunt the heavens and the plains
Whirled in a vortex that shall bring
The world to that destructive fire
Which burns before the ice-cap reigns. (CPP, 124–25)

In this cosmology, the war of constellations whirls about the eternal fire that ultimately closes it in destruction. The image recalls the "dancing around the bonfire" of the preceding section and foreshadows, in the fifth section of "East Coker," the fire, which is

. . . Not the intense moment
Isolated, with no before and after,
But a lifetime burning in every moment
And not the lifetime of one man only
But of old stones that cannot be deciphered. (CPP, 129)

Although the fire figure "betokeneth concorde" in "East Coker I" and the similar figure signifies war in "East Coker II," the "burning" in "East Coker V" disturbs the identity of the earlier figures as indexes of closure. This fire recalls the unreadability of all "old stones" and thereby draws attention to the essential difference in which concord is, like incarnation, an impossible problem.

The renunciation in "East Coker II" is similarly unsettling as it undercuts the "worn-out poetical fashion" that stands at its opening. A critique of knowledge as a cognitive core discernible within the differences of poetry, it marks such knowledge and the serenity or security achieved by its acquisition as a "receipt for deceit," a "deliberate hebetude" based upon an imposed, falsifying pattern. Such knowledge here looks like a Stevensian improvisation in the theater of trope or like the practical solutions of Eliot's dissertation that suggest no ultimate justification. We also recall here the impositions that Tom Sawyer's romantic dramas make on the unchartable flowing of *Huckleberry Finn* and recognize in this section of "East Coker II" Eliot's earlier challenge to such romantic cosmologies of closure, which are blind to the "new and shocking / Valuation" of every moment, to the constituting difference or the continual revaluation that endlessly multiplies patterns while undoing the ultimate justification for them all. This undoing, the estranging of knowledge from a universal and changeless core of transcendent truth, suggests that all knowledge is strictly differential, methodological, and improvised. Thus we are left with "the intolerable wrestle / With words and meanings," the difference that opens and reopens the seminal adventure of writing. This eternal return of difference leaves us once again

> In the middle, not only in the middle of the way
> But all the way, in a dark wood, in a bramble,
> On the edge of a grimpen, where is no secure foothold,
> And menaced by monsters, fancy lights,
> Risking enchantment. (CPP, 125)

Since the middle is "all the way," there is no way but the middle, the interminable faring forward of a poetry that always risks "enchantment" by an imposed pattern of knowledge while simultaneously eroding the illusory security of any firm foothold that can be taken as a reconciling chart, a reading or interpretation, of its transfigurative voyage in signs. *Huckleberry Finn*'s river is a similar critique of footholds, of the cognitive core Nietzsche calls the "firm" and Stevens the "bottom," and thus also redeploys the differential energy of poetry's seminal adventure.

"East Coker" opens with *Four Quartets*' most concise citation of the "worn-out poetical fashion" that understands difference as reducible to a core of identity: Mary's motto, "In my beginning is my end," a statement that asserts a controlling determinism to the history of the queen's life and thus illustrates the sacramental reading style that interprets history as subservient to a meaningful end (CPP, 123). The section then recounts the discontinuities and displacements of a history in which

> Houses rise and fall, crumble, are extended,
> Are removed, destroyed, restored, or in their place
> Is an open field, or a factory, or a by-pass. (CPP, 123)

By the end of this strophe, the firm certainty of its opening has been shaken by the repeated revaluations and differences of time that have made its story of a determining core into a "tattered arras woven with a silent motto." Although the written and fabricated motto assumes a determining direction or pattern to the warp and woof of history, Eliot's use of it here cites only its tattered wear, interrupting its motto as a no longer satisfactory "way of putting it" (CPP, 125). Like Hamlet, who in Act III, Scene iv of Shakespeare's play breaches the concealing arras to kill the king (who turns out to have been only a stand-in for a king who has himself displaced a dead father), Eliot's citation is here a knife that cuts into the fabrications of a sacramental hermeneutics to disclose and thus murder the king (the fictive pattern) that the discourse pretends is concealed by history's differences. When "East Coker" closes with a reversal of its opening line, "In my end is my beginning," it marks ends and beginnings, like the headwaters and deltas of rivers, as sites of difference and thus suggests the improvised and fabricated nature of beginnings and ends in general (CPP, 129). The strategic reversal intervenes in the discourse in which beginnings and ends are viewed as secure footholds in writing's river and discloses such stepping stones as sandbars emerging from the river itself and therefore subject to sudden effacement and displacement.

The "receipt for deceit" in "East Coker II" recalls another scene of concealment and deception, the one with which *Four Quartets* opens in "Burnt Norton I." Here the poet perceives the "formal pattern" in the "first world" of the garden, a perception of a fitfully recognized order in "Time present and time past" that seems to verify the poem's assertions elsewhere of such an organization to history (CPP, 117–18). But with an almost Stevensian trick, the poem interrupts this perception and the pattern it affirms through the mediations in which it is staged. The words of the poem here function like Stevens' echoes and are troped by the footfalls that

. . . echo in the memory
Down the passage which we did not take
Towards the door we never opened
Into the rose-garden. (CPP, 117)

Since "My words echo / Thus, in your mind," these lines describe the way words work, as pure noise with no rectifying message, or as echoes of a voicing that never occurred, and thus as disaffected echoes of a cognitive core that remains "a perpetual possibility / Only in a world of speculation." They repeat the problematic nature of such a core while nevertheless referring to it as though it were a determined essence only now concealed in the world of time and space. These words are sourceless echoes whose origin emerges as another improvisation of echoes. "Burnt Norton I" thus begins by repeating the differential energy of words.

Encouraged by the "deception of the thrush," itself an echo of the romantic imagination, the poem follows some of these echoes into the garden, which turns out to be not the site of their actual origin but rather a scene of hallucination and sleight-of-hand deceit. It is within this scene that the "formal pattern" is discovered, and here also that the sunlight illuminates only the mirage of water that stands in, as a disaffected visual echo, for the water that is actually not there. From this mirage of water, however, arises the phallic "lotos," this section's most apparent image of a core of transcendent identity. But its raising up, like an Apollonian illusion, occurs only in the mediation of a hallucination-inducing sunlight. The blinding influence of this sunlight stages the mirroring surface of the water, which, in turn, reflects a "heart of light" that, if looked at closely, reveals itself to be only a visual interference that blinds the perceiver to the actual emptiness of the pool. "Burnt Norton I" has thus followed echoes sustained by other echoes, which stand in for and supplement the first words that have never been spoken, concealing this absence in the blinding glitter of a mirage. The search, however, for the origin of the echoes—for the clear message in the differential noise of words—discloses this absence and its supplement, the reality of which "human kind / Cannot bear very much." This disclosure—"Then a cloud passed, and the pool was empty"—interrupts the vision of the garden as origin. It functions like memory in the dissertation, which interferes with the diseased hallucination of identity, thus redeploying a differential health and revealing the freedom that energizes the poem's transfigurative dance.

A similar disclosure results from another staging that occurs later in *Four Quartets*, the confrontation of the poet with the "familiar compound ghost" in "Little Gidding II" (CPP, 140). Emerging in a problematically duplicitous time,

> In the uncertain hour before the morning
>   Near the ending of interminable night
>   At the recurrent end of the unending, (CPP, 140)

the ghost appears first as an irreducibly compound figure of difference that cannot be reconciled with a core of identity, since it is "Both one and many . . . Both intimate and unidentifiable." As in *Hamlet*, which Eliot had earlier termed a problem because its main character "is dominated by an emotion which is inexpressible, because it is in *excess* of the facts as they appear," this ghost (a citation of Hamlet's father) deploys a similar difference that marks the staged conversation as a scene of ventriloquism (SW, 101). This scene, while it appears to reduce the excessive difference of the ghost and render his identity finally determinate ("What! are *you* here?"), also compounds that difference by doubling the poet's voice into two echoing segments ("I . . . cried / And heard another's voice cry") and his "being" into a site of difference ("I was still the same, / Knowing myself yet being someone other"). It repeats the difference that it was designed, as a staging of a conversation "between two worlds," to span or reduce. The determinate recognition achieved here thus discloses itself as only an improvisation fabricated by the rhetoric in which the scene is staged, for "the words sufficed / To compel the recognition they preceded."

The compulsive desire of speech to close itself upon a resolving core of identity (Stevens' human wish) is rehearsed by the ghost/poet himself:

> . . . our concern was speech, and speech impelled us
> To purify the dialect of the tribe
> And urge the mind to aftersight and foresight. (CPP, 141)

A purified dialect would be a language devoid of difference, one mastered by proper speech and spanned by a logic of cause and effect in which "aftersight" reveals speech's origin and foresight discloses its end. Such a speech is, therefore, chartable and readable, for the tension and decaying imprecision of its words vanish in the resolving stillness of their purity and the revelation of their truth (CPP, 141). These pure words would not dance, except to the choreography of the logic of aftersight and foresight.

But "there is only the dance" of words' unchartable differential energy, which is repeated again here in "Little Gidding II" as words impel us to seek their purity and closure only with a scene framed, like the Danish homeland Stevens uses in "The Auroras" to trope a pure principle, by compounded disaffection and difference. Thus the results of such an instinctive desire for purity can only be the "bitter tastelessness of shadow fruit" (recall the fictive fructification of "The Dry Salvages III" and the "husk of meaning" of "Little Gidding I"), the "conscious impotence of rage / At human folly," and the "rending pain of re-enactment," of the repeated quest for a purified language that is itself only a seductive fiction improvised with originally impure, dancing words. Such a quest, like Crispin's or that of the "time-ridden faces," proceeds "From wrong to wrong" and leads to a frustrated exasperation of the spirit, unless, the ghost/

poet concludes, the spirit is "restored by that refining fire / Where you must move in measure, like a dancer." The return of the fire image here recalls the "burning in every moment . . . of old stones that cannot be deciphered," a fire of liberating openness and un-readability that frees words from any pure essence of literal meaning. The spirit is restored in the disclosure of difference, which intervenes in the cataleptic effects of an endlessly frustrated desire or a sacramental hermeneutics, reminding us, like the Eumenides in *The Family Reunion* or the "difficultest rigor" in "Notes," of the differential, dancing being of all things. This restoration of the spirit redeploys the healthy differential energy of life; and, therefore, as "East Coker IV" states, "Our only health is the disease" of dis-ease, the transfigurative, energetic dance that is the repeated restoration of poetry's spirit (CPP, 129, 127). In staging the conversation with the ghost/poet, "Little Gidding II" dramatizes the difference between the two interpretations of words and writing out of which *Four Quartets* emerges, the difference "Little Gidding's" third section summarizes as the problematic of history, which may be the story of either servitude or freedom. This second section, however, rejects the "laughter at what ceases to amuse"—the exasperation of the constantly frustrated quest for closure and servitude—for a Nietzschean reaffirmation of the dance itself and of the differential freedom of words.

Whereas *Four Quartets* rejects the despairing interpretation of the ever-failing quest for words' closure and stillness, it affirms the freely circulating, transfigurative movement of poetry in which metaphor is endlessly displaced and replaced by other metaphor. It is a movement whose beginning is always already begun, since each origin is itself a metaphor staged as though it were a literal, non-metaphoric source of all metaphors, and whose end is perpetually deferred, since any ending appears, like any origin, only as a staging of metaphor. In this affirmation we see the influence Eliot the dissertation semiologist has on Eliot the theologian, who, in *The Waste Land* and *Murder in the Cathedral*, obscures the determination of difference that characterizes the dissertation's readings of Peirce and the transfigurative dance of *Four Quartets*. In the transfigurative dance of metaphor, a reconciling cognitive core can be thought only along with the interference of its production as another metaphoric improvisation or, in Stevens' phrase, as "Another image at the end of the cave" (CP, 411). There is, for both Eliot and Stevens, in the river of language and writing no privileged and secure place to stand, no cognitive foothold that is not another unstable sandbar, another improvised truth, that discloses the caprice of its contrivance. For both of these poets, language is a dynamically open and homeorrhetic system in which difference eternally returns and the erosion of firm, cognitive footholds never ends.

An epigraph would appear to be such a foothold, and *Four Quartets* opens with the citation of two fragments from Heraclitus. Critics have taken these epigraphs as summary statements of the argument of *Four Quartets* and therefore as prefatory remarks standing above the bar that marks the real beginning of the poem. But the very presence of the epigraphs, apparent still points of meaning and closure, multiplies the poem's actual beginning (does it begin with the first line of text, or with the epigraphs that precede it? with the title "Burnt Norton" or the title *Four Quartets*? or with the blank page that passes between the two titles?) to the point that no pure beginning can be affirmed with security, since each asserted beginning can be only a methodological imposition, a point taken to be a beginning by an interpretation. Eliot's use of epigraphs thus demonstrates the illimitable horizon of the river of metaphor whose "pure" beginning can only be cited as a pretense fabricated out of the fragments of a book that was itself pieced together by writers whose names may not have been Heraclitus. "Heraclitus . . . won his adherents by the fascination of his lapidary 'sayings,' the collection of which in the form of a book might not even have been made by himself, but only after his death."[13] Footholds in such a labyrinth of differing fragments can only be methodological improvisations or metaphoric sandbars. The Heraclitus citations get *Four Quartets* moving, deploying the differential energy of its dancing writing by disclosing the indecipherable openness of its beginning.

The poetic quest for a literal beginning to history and writing, in other words, always repeats the same disclosure. The quest is summarized in the question that ends the first strophe of "Little Gidding I."[14]

13. Felix M. Cleve, *The Giants of Pre-Socratic Greek Philosophy: An Attempt to Reconstruct Their Thoughts* (2 vols.; The Hague, 1973), I, 32.

14. Helen Gardner, *The Composition of Four Quartets* (London, 1978), 160, note to lines 19–20.

Where is the summer, the unimaginable
Summer beyond sense, the inapprehensible

Zero summer?

Asked again in the disaffected, suspended time "between pole
and tropic . . . Between melting and freezing"—the time of the
"pentecostal fire" of words' indecipherable difference in "East
Coker V"—the question incites another ancient cycle of desire for
the grounding "Zero summer" that remains deferred as "inapprehensible." But no matter what direction the reader takes—"If
you came this way, / Taking the route you would be likely to take,"
or "If you came at night," or "If you came by day"—"It would be
the same." The returning "same" here is marked by the "dull façade / And the tombstone" that the fifth section describes as the
"illegible stone" from which we start (CPP, 144). The returning
"same" is the redeployment of the difference that erodes the footholds of meaning and intentionality.

. . . And what you thought you came for
Is only a shell, a husk of meaning
From which the purpose breaks only when it is fulfilled
If at all. (CPP, 139)

The reader's arrival at his destination reveals not a core of meaning
but a shell that stands as a sign of its own hollowness and, therefore, of the vacuity at the center of summer's "zero." Although the
quest's aim is closure and the presentation of the inapprehensible
"beyond" of the senses, that very purpose repeats the destabilizing
difference that incited the search in the beginning, for

. . . Either you had no purpose
Or the purpose is beyond the end you figured
And is altered in fulfillment. (CPP, 139)

The reader's journey ends not in verification, instruction, information, or reportage but in the blind affirmation of a site "Where
prayer has been valid," the site of a ritualized language, like "Shan-
tih" at the end of *The Waste Land,* that is a problematic sign of the
deferral (in this case, into the past) of its ultimate validity. Prayer
emerges from "Little Gidding I" as a supplementary rhetoric standing in for a "Zero summer" that remains inapprehensible, thus disclosing its own essential heterogeneity.

A similar disclosure is recited by the figure of the "ragged rock" in "The Dry Salvages II," a figure that recalls the "insoluble lump" of "The Comedian." Unlike "Little Gidding I," which is a quest for a pure origin, "The Dry Salvages II" seeks an "end to the drifting wreckage," to improvised cognitive systems, tossed up, as "The Dry Salvages I" indicated, by the uncontrollably differential force of the river and the sea. This wreckage was of the artifacts constructed to bridge or control the sea's pulsatory energy, but "The Dry Salvages II" desires a stable and justifiable cognitive core for the drifting wreckage of words, which "crack" and "break" and which, like sandbars in a river, "will not stay in place / Will not stay still" (CPP, 133, 121). What the poem discloses, however, is that each desired end to the verbal drift is only another addition, another piece of wreckage that does not end the differential energy of the stream of words but rather, like a Peircean object, redeploys it. "The Dry Salvages II" affirms a "final addition" that is itself a parody of finality, since it emerges within "a drifting boat with a slow leakage," and thus can only figuratively end the drift and the wreckage that determines its appearance. In seeking an end to this verbal wreckage in a cognitive core, the first four strophes reveal that

> We cannot think of a time that is oceanless
> Or of an ocean not littered with wastage
> Or of a future that is not liable
> Like the past, to have no destination. (CPP, 132)

Like Stevens, who looks back at the world only from a point already within a sea of improvised transformations and suggests that it has no identity except in these different improvisations, Eliot here suggests that we are always adrift in a sea littered with difference—different meanings, different truths, different cognitive systems—and devoid of a destination in a rectifying harbor of identity.

The end of such a drift, then, can only be an improvised foothold fabricated from and within the verbal stream to give words the illusion of a stable cognitive core and their differential significances the pretense of a destination in a literal truth. "We have to think of them," Eliot writes, "as forever bailing . . . Or drawing their money, drying sails at dockage"; we have to think of the voyage of writing as having a destination, a payoff that redeems the drift for coinage of real value. But the words "we have to think" have the ring of desperate coercion about them, and, indeed, the story of destination and redemption is told only after this section's disclosure of the illimitably directionless drift of words. It is this seductive story of the voyage's closure, a history of the redeemability of verbal drift, that obscures a second story of the voyage of words, which is told after the semicolon of the fourth strophe. In this story, words make "a trip that will be unpayable / For a haul that will not bear examination." By characterizing the verbal voyage as ultimately unredeemable in anything but more words, Eliot interrupts the trip by doubling its history as both servitude (closure) and freedom (openness). This second story of liberated drift is the one affirmed by the Krishna citation of the next section.

"Behind the assurance / Of recorded history"—behind, that is, the patterned hermeneutics of the closed book in which words always arrive at their meaningful destinations—lies the difference of the ineffable that the book cannot account for, the difference that emerges from history as a "primitive terror," that erodes the book's assurance of closure.

> We had the experience but missed the meaning,
> And approach to the meaning restores the experience
> In a different form, beyond any meaning
> We can assign to happiness. (CPP, 133)

There can be no assurance of identity or meaning in such a differential history. Recorded history, then, "ceases to be a mere sequence" but rather appears also as the redeployment of an ineffable difference and, therefore, as a commentary upon the illusion of a recordable history, of the differences of time closed in a cognitive core.[15] The "ragged rock"—a sign of a firm foothold of reconciling, justifiable meaning in the "restless waters" of the verbal drift—is finally joined to the other wreckages (the "cargo of dead Negroes, cows and chicken coops") by the emphatic positioning of the conjunction *and*. Appearing at some times as a "monument" and at others as a "seamark," the rock seems to be a secure point of reference within the liquid slippage of words. But "in the sombre season," it is disclosed as "what it always was": a mark of the ineffable, whose identity can never be other than locally unstable and essentially uncertain. The ragged rock manifests the eternal return of difference.

15. *Ibid.*, 132, note to line 102.

It is from this mark of difference and unreadability, this "illegible stone" that repeatedly recalls the unbridgeable and irreducibly differential character of the river of writing, that, as "Little Gidding V" finally has it, "we start." This beginning in difference and freedom always returns to erode the securely servile hermeneutics of identity and closure. It is a beginning always already begun, since there is no beginning that is not also the site of an illegible interference. "What we call the beginning is often the end / And to make an end is to make a beginning." The citation of a beginning involves a calling, a naming, a fabrication, or making that finally recalls its fabrication, thereby disclosing the intervention by which a beginning emerges within writing's differential wreckage only as a point of improvisation and interference. The reiteration of the essential heterogeneity of the call or the name redeploys the difference essential to writing. "Every phrase and every sentence is an end and a beginning," a closure to, or final patterning of, words' drifting wreckage that can be never other than a pretense, since it is simultaneously a beginning, another faring forward in the verbal stream itself. *Four Quartets* always finds itself adrift in an illimitable sea of disaffected metaphor and illegible words, and thus "Every poem is an epitaph," like the "stele" in "The Auroras of Autumn," to the rock of a cognitive core irreversibly eroded by the differential energy of writing (CPP, 144; CP, 417). We start—again and always— at sea in words, in the "pentecostal fire" of writing's differential energy. We begin with writing, with the improvisational action of "calling" that always recalls words' cognitive core as the site of the "so-called," the site of fabrication, difference, and metaphor.

Four Quartets ends with such a recollection, a discovery of "the last of earth left to discover"—namely, "that which was the beginning," the "source of the longest river." It is a recollection that calls the source the half-heard "voice of the hidden waterfall," a site of noise and interference, and affirms its emergence in "the stillness / Between two waves of the sea"—in, that is, the pulsing waves of difference. The naming of the source discloses the originating difference in which the so-called source emerges, and the poem concludes with the recitation of this differential freedom that defers into a future "Never here to be realised" the entropic closure of words (CPP, 145, 136).

And all shall be well and
All manner of thing shall be well

When the tongues of flame are in-folded
Into the crowned knot of fire
And the fire and the rose are one. (CPP, 145)

The anxiety about difference that motivates Eliot's sacramental hermeneutics becomes, in *Four Quartets,* an affirmation of difference and of the energetic, differential life of writing and cognition. Eliot infuses the static rhetoric of Christianity with the dynamics of difference—his incarnation is a site of difference, his pentecostal fire the redeployment of differential energy. His model of writing is the interminable voyage, the endless adventure, the faring forward between different, incommensurable cognitive constructs with no core of identity or resolution, between, that is, the instrumental or methodological truths of what looks like a Jamesian pluralistic universe. It is this lateral drift between metaphors that is finally affirmed in Eliot. This affirmation interferes with the desire of the sacramental hermeneutics—the desire for the end of difference in the revelation of identity—so apparent in other of his texts and makes him sound, strangely enough, like Stevens, enjoying the pleasure of merely circulating that characterizes the health of poetry.

For Stevens, difference also suggests the constituting energy of writing and thinking. His poetic voyages are farings forward that rely upon endless differentiations, upon an infinite series of *and yet*'s whose end, like the underpattern in Eliot, the object in Peirce, or the firm in Nietzsche, can only be another methodological improvisation, a speculative metaphor that itself suggests the eternal return of difference. Difference in Stevens appears as the origin of thought, as the operator that produces the things that are different, and as the repeated procedure that constitutes the being of all things. Stevens' poetry does not oscillate between two independent poles of experience—the imagination and reality, the self and the world, the subjective and the objective. Rather, it emphasizes the differential relationships in which these oppositions are originally constituted. What counts in Stevens is the differentiating process, not the interfering identities it produces. Stevens' poetry reflects an Eliotic differential energy, a dynamics of difference that constitutes its homeorrhetic, open life.

Six
Methodology and the Dynamics of Difference

With its often reflexively philosophic rhetoric, Stevens' poetry invites critical discussions of metaphor that seek to distinguish between metaphoric practice and a theory of metaphor, a generalized law of this practice, that accounts literally for the poems' endlessly metaphoric elaborations. A glance at a list of Stevens' titles reveals the extent of his concern with metaphor and his desire to make literal statements about the metaphors he writes. From the early "Metaphors of a Magnifico" through the later poems "The Motive for Metaphor," "Thinking of a Relation between the Images of Metaphors," and "Metaphor as Degeneration," Stevens' poetry repeatedly returns to metaphor as the subject or tenor carried by its metaphorical vehicles. As one "Adagia" entry states, "It is only *au pays de la métaphore qu'on est poète*," and it often appears to be Stevens' intention to chart the boundaries and describe the terrain of that metaphorical *pays* (OP, 179). This poetry, then, is a strangely complicated one that is itself a meta-metaphorics, a commentary about metaphor nevertheless written with metaphors. A difference is always suggested by this commentary—a difference between, for example, a metaphor's vehicle and its tenor, between the figurative statement and its literal significance (metaphor and meta-metaphor), or between poetry and critical meta-language. This difference, however, is never secure in Stevens, where difference is deployed as a problem that interferes with the apparently privileged status of the prefix *meta-*, the "designation for a higher science . . . of the same nature [as its subject] but dealing with ulterior and more fundamental problems." [1] At risk in Stevens, as it is in *Four Quartets,* is the security of the neutral and the literal, of the omniscient observer-elect and the line that separates commentary and theory from poetry and practice.

The "ease of mind" that opens Stevens' late meditation on metaphor, "Prologues to What Is Possible," is the subject or tenor carried forward in that poem's opening canto by the metaphor of the boat journey, like those of *Four Quartets* and "The Comedian as the Letter C," of a vessel and its passenger sailing toward a "point of central arrival" (CP, 516). Metaphor has classically been described as a programmed voyage, communication, or transportation of its literal tenor from one place or word to another. Aristotle states that metaphor consists "in giving the thing a name that belongs to something else; the transference being either from genus to species, or from species to genus, or from species to species, or on grounds of analogy." Furthermore, he exemplifies the transportation of "the thing" from "genus to species" with a nautical figure from the *Odyssey:* "'Here stands my ship'; for lying at anchor is the 'standing' of a particular kind of thing." [2] In Stevens' poem, the vessel that carries the thing, that names "an ease of mind" with a "name that belongs to something else," is the sea voyage that ends with a safe arrival at its destination. It is, even more specifically, the metaphor of metaphor as a directed and orderly transference. Unlike the faring forward or the lateral drift of *Four Quartets,* this metaphoric voyage is the story of metaphor's arrival at a safe haven of literal meaning. Here is no haphazard or improvised voyage, for even the medium through which the vessel of metaphor travels seems to know where it is going.

> There was an ease of mind that was like being alone in a boat at sea,
> A boat carried forward by waves resembling the bright backs of rowers,
> Gripping their oars, as if they were sure of the way to their destination.
>   (CP, 515)

1. Oxford English Dictionary, compact ed., s.v. "meta-."
2. Aristotle, *Rhetoric and Poetics of Aristotle,* trans. W. Rhys Roberts and Ingram Bywater (New York, 1954), 251.

The voyage is not without some degree of risk, for the vessel's passenger feels himself "lured on by a syllable without any meaning," but this provisional meaninglessness, this momentary drift of the vessel of metaphor, will finally come about when it is revealed to have been under control all along—when, that is, the "point of central arrival," the end of the journey in the conveyance of its meaning, is achieved (CP, 516). This is the passenger's faith in the steerage of the vessel, in the

> . . . syllable of which he felt, with an appointed sureness,
> That it contained the meaning into which he wanted to enter,
> A meaning which, as he entered it, would shatter the boat and leave the
>   oarsmen quiet. (CP, 516)

In its arrival at its destination, the voyage of metaphor ends, and the vessel that has carried the passenger to this center—and even the medium through which the voyage has taken place—shatters and reaches a point of stillness and silence. Having done its job, the vessel of metaphor effaces itself into nothingness; its difference collapses to identity, and thus it presents without interruption the central meaning that was its destination all along.

But a strange digression comes between this metaphor's tenor, which opens the canto, and its vehicle, the journey most fully articulated at the canto's closing. At the center of the metaphor of the voyage is another metaphor, that of the floating vessel itself, the critical figure in terms of which the metaphoric voyage toward meaning is written. This metaphor of metaphor, as a vessel bearing its contents, or the vehicle its passenger or tenor, is disturbed here, for the metaphoric boat turns out to be an uncontrollably floating vessel in which the simple opposition, the determination of the difference, between containing vehicle and contained tenor becomes a problem. In Stevens' writing of this classical metaphor of metaphor, the nautical vehicle contains the "he" that it conveys, but at the same time this "he" contains the vessel for which he himself becomes the vehicle, or symbol. Here is the problematic center of the canto:

> He belonged to the far-foreign departure of his vessel and was part of it,
> Part of the speculum of fire on its prow, its symbol, whatever it was,
> Part of the glass-like sides on which it glided over the salt-stained water.
>   (CP, 516)

The "he" is inside the vessel as its contents, but "he" is also outside the vessel as its symbol. In this figure, the simple opposition be-

tween vehicle and tenor, vessel and contents, outside symbol and inside symbolized, becomes an unsolvable problem, for both terms
uncontrollably shift places in a perplexingly interreferential relationship, a "speculum" of mirrorings. In this relationship the identity of the vehicle cannot finally be distinguished from that of the
tenor, and thus metaphor's voyage is set adrift from the inside by its
own vessel, the classical metaphor of metaphor that, as Stevens
writes it, interferes with Aristotle's categories and deploys metaphor itself as a problem.

Like burglary for Eliot, this problematic drift is not, for Stevens,
a condition of bad metaphor or of a poorly constructed vehicle that
simply fails to arrive at its destination, for the classical metaphor of
metaphor, the boat itself,

> . . . was built of stones that had lost their weight and being no longer
> heavy
> Had left in them only a brilliance, of unaccustomed origin,
> So that he that stood up in the boat leaning and looking before him
> Did not pass like someone voyaging out of and beyond the familiar.
>   (CP, 515)

The vessel of metaphor is constituted as a weightless structure that,
like Nietzsche's edifice of cobwebs, is a "brilliance, of unaccustomed
origin," an auroral effulgence with no weighty, substantial core. Its
drift is an always already begun voyage (like Crispin's or as in *Four
Quartets*) with no determinable point of origin, no familiar haven
that it voyages "out of and beyond." Its departure, like the land's
end we look back on from a sea of transformations, can only be recalled as different, unaccustomed, and "far-foreign." And its end in
a "point of central arrival" is, as indicated above, of necessity deferred, an observation also suggested by the verb tense in which the
story of metaphor's arrival is written. This voyage traces a lateral
sliding, an almost Eliotic faring forward, that, like the river in
Huckleberry Finn or Peirce's infinite regression of signs, can have
only improvised beginning and ending points.

According to Aristotle, the drifting vessel of metaphor is righted
and brought under control by a kinship or natural likeness that ties
vehicle to tenor, thereby assuring a complete communication and a
successful voyage. As he states in the *Rhetoric*, in a passage about
the use of metaphors, "We must draw them not from remote but
from kindred and similar things, so that the kinship is clearly perceived as soon as the words are said." This comment elaborates on

his earlier observation that "metaphors . . . must be fitting, which means that they must fairly correspond to the thing signified."[3] This correspondence between signifier and signified keeps metaphor from what Aristotle calls conspicuous "inappropriateness"—that is, from drifting away from and thereby obscuring the meaning it is intended to convey and from calling attention to its difference *as metaphor.* The vehicle of metaphor, for Aristotle, is thus guided by resemblance, and the pleasure we feel upon hearing or reading metaphors comes from our perception of the ways in which both vehicle and tenor are the same. It is a pleasure derived from the recognition of identity in difference.

It is the significance of this guiding likeness and the meaning of the "same" itself that the second canto of "Prologues to What Is Possible" speculates upon. The canto opens not with an assertion of a natural likeness between the vehicle and tenor but with a fearful assertion of their essential heterogeneity. "The object with which he was compared / Was beyond his recognizing" (CP, 516). By this difference, by the absence of a perceivable identity the metaphor communicates, "he knew that likeness of him extended / Only a little way, and not beyond." The first canto's metaphor of metaphor, itself a citation of the trope by which metaphor is characterized in classical rhetoric, thus appears here not as a difference between a vehicle and a tenor joined by the reconciling thread of an identity, but as a differentiation in which the "same" of natural kinship always fails to appear. Metaphor cannot, therefore, be said to be guided by likeness and resemblance, by the re-presentation of the "same" in the different, but must rather be seen to put at risk the identity from which likeness and resemblance seem to be derived. No identity collapses the difference between tenor and vehicle (which are themselves problematic sites of difference), and without this anchoring line of resemblance, without a core of identity whose communication overcomes difference, the voyage of metaphor must be an interminable drift; a seminal adventure or Odyssean wandering subject to no "point of central arrival," but only to incidental accident and chance.

Here is where the "same" is reinscribed in metaphor, but with a different significance:

3. *Ibid.,* 170, 168.

. . . unless between himself
And things beyond resemblance there was this and that intended to be
  recognized,
The this and that in the enclosures of hypotheses
On which men speculated in summer when they were half asleep.
  (CP, 516)

In this elaboration of Stevens' metaphor of metaphor, an identity does in fact appear (the figure of the "this and that intended to be recognized"), but it arises as a consequence of a methodological intention and comes as a supplement to "what was real and its vocabulary" (CP, 517). It incites resemblance, but only under the auspices of a contrived and supplemental identity, only, that is, under the mark of an intentionality that seeks to efface the essential heterogeneity of metaphor by a supplementary device. And this supplementary "same" cannot finally resolve the difference in which it is written, for although it is intended to be that which is recognized—the unifying identity that anchors a metaphoric vehicle in a central meaning—it nevertheless remains within the "enclosures of hypotheses" as a point of speculation. It is an identity that, because its nature is speculative, is never the "point of central arrival" but the redeployment of a problem. Thus, although the Stevensian metaphor of metaphor ultimately repeats the Aristotelian figure of resemblance as a repetition of metaphor as the re-presentation of identity, it does so only by skewing that identity, deploying it as a site of difference or purely hypothetical speculation. In Stevens as in Eliot, the voyage of metaphor may never pay off for anything other than more metaphors.

If the "same" is, as the poem characterizes it, an insecure supplement added to an originally centerless field of differences, then the very idea of recognition, of the perception of the "same" the supplemental "this and that" are intended to produce, suggests a significance different from the one associated with it by classical rhetoric. There, recognition is structured upon a spatializing or temporalizing difference. It implies the knowing again, or the re-cognition in a different time or place, of some originally known identity. Re-cognition takes place only through the delay and difference that allows the same identity to be perceived twice, the first time properly in itself (cognition) and the second time in something different (recognition). But re-cognition in Stevens' poem interferes with this classical definition, for it cannot be said to derive from an identity that is repeated. "The object with which he was compared," we recall, "was beyond his recognizing," and thus re-cognition describes neither the repetition of an original cognition nor the re-presentation of some identity, but the function of differentiation. A likeness between them can in fact be achieved only through the coercion of a methodological intention. Re-cognition in this poem is not derived from cognition, does not mark the second appearance of an original knowledge, because it deploys difference radically and irreducibly. For this reason, the hierarchical opposition that ties recognition to cognition, difference to identity, no longer makes sense, for recognition is constituted as an essential heterogeneity that can be reduced to an identity only through the mediation of an improvised and supplemental intention that calls attention to its own desire for such identity. This poem negates any Aristotelian kinship between objects or metaphors. It insists upon the difference that constitutes both recognitions and cognitions, upon the relationship of difference in which they *are* as things that are different. The field of knowledge, then, is insistently multiple, and it functions through differences and differentiations, not through the re-presentation of a central identity; it is the operator of difference that produces knowledge differentially and multiply. Difference comes first, and as the poem's title suggests, there are only the multiple "Prologues to What Is Possible" that are spoken either before or in place of a central *logos* whose identity they both introduce and displace. These prologues describe a field of difference that constitutes the differential being of *logos*.

A constituting difference structures the argument of Stevens' 1937 essay, "The Irrational Element in Poetry," in which the poet meditates upon the apparently fallen nature of poetic language and the *via negativa* by which the recognition of the fictive nature of words seems to disclose a truth beyond the horizons of fiction and metaphor, to reveal, that is, a truly transcendent identity the essay names equally the "irrational" and the "unknown." It is, in other words, the distinctiveness of poetry from this identity that suggests its absolute transcendence. Here, apparently, is a clear indication of Stevens' place in what has been called the "conservative fictionalist tradition of modern poetics and philosophy," which, like a type of negative theology, understands language as an always inadequate representation of an essential truth that transcends the constraining and limiting horizon of words.[4] And yet this limiting horizon is, in Stevens, a line that can never be securely drawn; the difference between poetic metaphor and transcendent truth, like that between vehicle and tenor in metaphor, cannot finally be determined. In this essay, the difference between the fictive "known" and the true "unknown" or, for Eliot, the difference between accident and intention in poetry, structures the argument but at the same time suggests its strictly methodological and ultimately unjustifiable significance (OPP, 13).

After some introductory remarks, the essay opens with an anecdote: the story of a snowy Thanksgiving in Hartford and of the poet, lying in bed, hearing "the steps of a cat running over the snow under [his] window almost inaudibly." This sound becomes for Stevens a figure of all meta-poetic "pretexts for poetry," of all sources lying behind or beyond poetic language, which, the essay later explains, the poet, "grows completely tired of" in an exhaustion that drives him toward a desired "subject." The anecdote of the poetic pretext begins to define the irrational as a "transaction between reality and the sensibility of the poet" that is the origin "from which poetry springs" (OP, 217, 221). This transaction assumes a clear differentiation between object and subject, reality and sensibility, and the ability of poetic language to mediate this difference.

The irrational that Stevens refers to in the essay also suggests this distinction, for it appears as an absolute transcendence to which the essay's language can only negatively refer. It suggests, for example, an identity named by its various names. As Stevens writes late in the essay, "I use the word irrational more or less indifferently, as between its several senses," since any single sense shows itself to be only an untrue metaphor of the irrational that can have no proper sensual image. Stevens here evades a definition of the irrational by multiplying its various senses, a strategy he uses again in "The Noble Rider and the Sound of Words," where he shows nobility "unfixed," because "if it is defined, it will be fixed and it must not be fixed. . . . To fix it is to put an end to it" (OP, 229; NA, 34). Like nobility, the irrational appears as that which lies beyond words as an identity that language can indicate only by describing its own limitations—only, that is, by following a *via negativa* of

4. Frank Lentricchia, *After the New Criticism* (Chicago, 1980), 31.

self-deprecation. This critique of language thus would seem to disclose the truth of the irrational in the differences between its "several senses." In it the distinction between difference and identity seems to be clear.

Not to follow this road—not to self-consciously assert the fallen and restricted nature of language—results in a subreption that reduces the ideal identity of the irrational by rendering it a representable object within the horizon of writing. In "The Irrational Element in Poetry," Stevens refers to Freud as "one of the great figures in the world" and notes that "while he is responsible for very little in poetry . . . he has given the irrational a legitimacy that it never had before," perhaps by writing a discourse Freud presumes to be the accurate description of the irrational and not simply a disclosure of its methodological inadequacy. This favorable allusion to Freud and his book of the irrational turns hostile, however, five years later in "The Noble Rider and the Sound of Words," in which Stevens indicts Freud and Descartes as two of a "great many people" who have "cut poetry's throat" (OP, 218–19; NA, 14). It is the murderous subreption of Freud's discourse and, perhaps, the distinctiveness of the Cartesian subject and object that Stevens attacks. Since the irrational is, according to Stevens, an ideal identity that can never be properly named, its determination in any discourse must be a delusion akin to what Kant, using a similar logic with respect to the sublime, calls fanaticism. Stevens' fluctuating and unfixed "definition" of the irrational avoids this self-delusion by maintaining the irrational as the inexplicable and finally indescribable center of his essay. This definition that refuses to define is a self-conscious strategy that, by disclosing the fallen fictiveness of discourse, seeks to insure the exclusion of the irrational from writing and thus its protection from the contaminations of writing's fictions. Like the moment of Becket's decision in *Murder in the Cathedral,* the irrational appears as the silent identity at the heart of writing's inadequate definitions. The delineation of the difference between the definitions we know and the unknown truth of the irrational is a strategy necessary to the *via negativa* of conservative fictionalism, for it is only by articulating this difference that writing can mark itself as fiction and, at the same time, gesture toward an uncontaminated truth beyond itself. This distinction between writing and truth must be made, for it is only because of this difference that the identity of the irrational can be suggested.

And yet it is the justification for this difference that the essay finally calls into question. As the title of the essay reminds us, the irrational is never really a transcendent identity, since it is an irrational element *in* poetry, the name of a "particular process in the rational mind which we recognize as irrational in the sense that it takes place unaccountably." The irrational that Stevens has suggested is completely distinct from words and writing also, it now appears, has a function within them. Because it can be described as taking place neither strictly within language's contaminated inside nor strictly on its pure outside, the irrational, like Eliot's Eumenides or Stevens' auroras, deploys the insistent difference that destabilizes the simple binary oppositions between inside and outside, fictive language and pure pre-text. These clear distinctions, in other words, can have only a methodological, or strategic, significance. For Stevens, such methodological distinctions constitute an "unwritten rhetoric . . . to which the poet must always be turning" (OP, 218, 226). The repetition of this rhetoric, in which language and reality appear to be two distinct identities, is the unaccountable process that opens poetry. The "unwritten rhetoric" of poetry is this strategic redeployment of difference in which different things emerge. Poetry makes the distinctions, the differences, in which all things are; but these distinctions have no ultimate justification. They are, to use the figure of "The Auroras," always improvisations. It is the eternal return of this differentiating rhetoric, a differential energy like that of *Four Quartets,* that is for Stevens the pretext "from which poetry springs."

This unaccountable process of differentiation is crucial to the final section of "The Irrational Element in Poetry," which opens with the statement, "The irrational bears the same relation to the rational that the unknown bears to the known." What follows is an intricate description of the dynamics of the known, which Stevens equates to the dynamics of poetry. "I do not for a moment mean to indulge in mystical rhetoric, since for my part, I have no patience with that sort of thing. That the unknown as the source of knowledge, as the object of thought, is part of the dynamics of the known does not permit denial." The dynamics of the known repeats the differentiating process whereby two figures, the known and the unknown, are distinguished by a differentiating boundary that separates them; the citing of this boundary allows the unknown to be envisioned as individualized and differ ̤nt from the known. This boundary, however, is never rigorously determined and thus is never innocently neutral, since it is imposed by the "dynamics of the known," whose coercive force Stevens here describes as undeniable. To write or to think is to repeat this productive, differentiating rhetoric without which we can neither think nor write. As Stevens later observes, "We accept the unknown even when we are most skeptical" (OP, 227, 228). It is thus only from within this differentiating rhetoric, in which the distinctions that mark the appearance of individualized identities are improvised, that a figure of a transcendent source (the unknown, the irrational) ever emerges. The dynamics of the known is the product of the dynamics of difference.

The productive differentiating procedure is repeated by one of Stevens' adages concerning god and reality: "There is no such thing as a metaphor of a metaphor. One does not progress through metaphors. When I say that man is a god it is very easy to see that if I say god is something else, god has become reality" (OP, 179). This passage requires careful reading, for it turns on a particular problem arising within the first sentence. What is suggested by the observation that there cannot be a "metaphor of a metaphor"? The second sentence supplies a possible interpretation: "One does not progress through metaphor" to some outside of metaphor, to some privileged position not already inhabited by metaphor. The adage suggests that such a passage through metaphor is at the same time a circulation or a lateral drift within an illimitable field of metaphor whose horizon one never crosses. A meta-metaphorics, a writing on or about metaphor, necessarily proceeds only from within the metaphoric field; statements about metaphor must themselves be metaphoric statements. An outside to this circulation of metaphor represents, for Stevens, the unthinkable.

And yet within this lateral drift of metaphor a certain "reality," and, therefore, a type of margin distinguishing metaphor from its "indispensable element" do appear. But this reality does not take place at some privileged location beyond metaphor; it is not a transcendent identity outside of the metaphoric field in which it is represented. Rather, it appears as an effect produced by the passage of one metaphor into another and not as the final destination of an impossible voyage through metaphor and at which metaphor can be said to end. The passage of metaphor into metaphor produces a residue that we call "reality," Stevens' name for this indispensable effect of metaphoric circulation. This process has no nonrhetorical justification, for reality can always be called something else. What is indispensable in metaphor, therefore, is not a core of identity but rather the differentiating rhetoric, the structure of differences, in which the metaphoric and the essential can be spoken of as though they were distinctly individualized. A reality or a god is always improvised for metaphor (and vice versa) as a condition of its appearance. Thus the difference between figurative language and phenomenal reality, text and pre-text, metaphor and statements about metaphor, marks the return of a methodological procedure and not simply the articulation of two individualized identities, for these identities and their distinctiveness always turn out to be suspect.

In two late poems from *The Rock* this methodological procedure can also be traced. In "The Plain Sense of Things," Stevens recounts the "end of the imagination," a passing of the "great structure [that] has become a minor house." The imagination is here troped as a greenhouse, a place of artificial growth that metaphorically reflects the presumably natural growth that takes place on its outside. The first three stanzas nostalgically mark the decay and death of poetry and the return to a "plain sense of things." But this return to the plain is never other than a return to image and metaphor, for "the absence of the imagination had / Itself to be imagined." The final two stanzas invoke a literal reality in the figure of the "great pond, / The plain sense of it, without reflections," but they also suggest that this reality is already an imaginary artifice. This sense of the plain, of the unreflected or literal, is thus the "inevitable knowledge, / Required, as a necessity requires," by the greenhouse of metaphor as an "indispensable element," as the reality from which it can be distinguished. As Stevens writes in another "Adagia" entry, "reality is a cliché from which we escape by metaphor"; but it is the methodological cliché also repeated by metaphor (CP, 502; OP, 179). The "inevitable knowledge" of poetry marks the eternal return of reality as this cliché.

A similar cliché appears in "The Green Plant," a poem that, like many of Stevens' other poems (particularly "The Auroras of Autumn"), recites the figure of the sun only to interfere with its Platonic identification as a sign of the transcendent, the literal, and the pure ideal (CP, 506). The poem opens by announcing the decay of the "effete vocabulary of summer," of a solar language that privileges a punctual and transcendent source of truth and enlightenment. This vocabulary, however, "No longer says anything." The "brown at the bottom of red" and the "orange far down in yellow," figures of a substantial, grounding depth, are disclosed to have been

> . . . falsifications from a sun
> In a mirror, without heat,
> In a constant secondariness,
> A turning down toward finality— (CP, 506)

The sun can no longer be spoken of as the literal center of all truth, for the subreption of its language has apparently been seen through. A reflection "without heat," the sun now appears not as the primary and original source of life but as a "constant secondariness," or a derivative cliché—that is, as a metaphor of a vocabulary that is effete.

But the final stanza of the poem begins with an apparent exception to this vocabulary, the green plant that "glares." This plant, a figure of the "harsh reality of which it is a part," is, however, no less a trope than the already decentered metaphor of the sun. It, too, is a "constant secondariness," for it appears only when one looks at the "legend of the maroon and olive forest." It is thus the legend's metaphor of its pre-text, of the "harsh reality" that it claims is outside of itself but which is never other than a figure produced within the text of the legend itself. In this manner, then, the difference between text and pre-text, contrived legend and harsh reality, cannot be rigorously determined; it allows for the articulation of both terms but negates the absolute identity of either by calling attention to their strictly methodological significance. The displacement of Platonic language by the green plant of phenomena traces not a passage from error to truth, metaphorical fiction to literal reality, but rather the lateral sliding in which one cliché of the "real" is substituted for another. In "The Plain Sense of Things" and "The Green Plant," as in all of Stevens' writings, "one does not progress through metaphor" to a "something else" over the horizon, since both the metaphoric and the literal emerge as the products of a differentiating rhetorical procedure.

Both of the voyages traced in Stevens' poems featuring the classical archetype of the "interminable adventurer," Ulysses, productively deploy this differentiating procedure. "The World as Meditation" focuses on the moment of Ulysses' return to Penelope in order to disclose in that moment the eternal return of difference. The poem only figuratively moves toward a resolution of the question that opens it, "Is it Ulysses that approaches from the east?" This question is marked by the horizon formed by Penelope's veiling "cretonnes." The horizon locates the apparent boundary between the artifice of composition (Penelope "has composed, so long a self with which to welcome his") and the reality figured as Ulysses' "savage presence."

   . . . Someone is moving

  On the horizon and lifting himself up above it.
  A form of fire approaches the cretonnes of Penelope,
  Whose mere savage presence awakens the world in which she dwells.
    (CP, 520)

This image of the form appearing on the horizon recalls an earlier poem, "A Primitive Like an Orb," in which the form is a "giant of nothingness" always evolved or produced by a discourse of desire as the sign of an ideal identity lying beyond its boundaries: "the obscurest as, the distant was" that is "always too heavy for the sense / To seize" (CP,441). But this giant is simply the "fated eccentricity" of "the lover, the believer and the poet," whose "words are chosen out of their desire."

  Here, then, is an abstraction given head,
  A giant on the horizon, given arms,
  A massive body and long legs, stretched out,
  A definition with an illustration, not
  Too exactly labeled, a large among the smalls
  Of it, a close, parental magnitude,
  At the centre on the horizon, concentrum, grave
  And prodigious person, patron of origins. (CP, 443)

We hear in this passage the Kantian sublime that binds up "with the representation a kind of respect, as also a kind of contempt for what we simply call 'small'"; but the Stevensian "giant," the echo of the Kantian "*absolutely great*," results from an interreferential relationship of poetic texts in which "one poem proves another" as a definition supported by an illustration.[5] The "giant, on the horizon"

---

5. Immanuel Kant, *Kant's Critique of Judgement*, trans. J. H. Bernard (London, 1914), 108.

seems to mark the border that distinguishes poetry from an ideal identity, but this giant is never other than an illusion disclosed as a part of the total "Of letters, prophecies, perceptions, clods, / Of color"—a part, that is, of the lateral drift of metaphor and a product of the differentiating procedure that structures it.

This interreferentiality of poems and metaphors intrudes upon even so fundamental an opposition as the difference between being and not-being, negating both terms while redeploying the difference that constitutes them. The giant who takes his place on the horizon "is and . . . Is not and, therefore, is." Like the irrational, his is a purely contradictory and differential being that interferes with the security of the categories of being and not-being and suggests the arbitrariness of such philosophical distinctions. Ulysses, another manifestation of the giant, suggests a similar negation in "The World as Meditation." His form both "was Ulysses and it was not," thus disclosing the purely improvisational nature of his identity. The meeting between "friend and dear friend," the return of Ulysses, is staged only by the repetition of the name that, by "never forgetting him that kept coming constantly so near," redeploys the differentiating procedure that produces the cliché of "mere savage presence."

The later poem, "The Sail of Ulysses," takes place within a framing horizon of italics that itself encloses another frame formed by quotation marks. The inside frame presumably marks the writing it circumscribes as the accurate transcription of the living voice of Ulysses, the speaker of the poem's central sections. It suggests that this writing recites, word for word, Ulysses' original speech, and thus it repeats the binary oppositions speech/writing, original voicing/ derived citation, presence/representation. But these oppositions, framed by the poem's italicized sections, are therefore already the result of a rhetorical or textual procedure. Among their other uses, italics, which constitute a strictly written device, function as signs indicating when language or writing is citing itself. For example, the word *knowledge,* when used to exemplify the grammatical category *noun,* would within a conventional typography be rendered in italics. Thus the poem opens a doubled citation; the quotation marks that cite Ulysses' original voice are themselves recited by the italicized sections that frame them as a citation of citation. The distinction between an original speech and its written citation takes place here only when surrounded by the italics with which writing quotes itself. It is therefore the consequence of this textual, even graphic, organization. Indeed, Ulysses' voice is itself a recitation of a certain writing, a text it repeats as this "*symbol of the seeker . . . read*[s] his own mind" (OP, 99). The poem recites the written recitation of a symbol reading writing. Here citation endlessly folds back on itself, interfering with, but producing as a rhetorical improvisation, an original voice. Citation cannot be said to be derived from an original source, nor can writing be understood as the representation of an original voice. "The Sail of Ulysses" figures an interminably drifting voyage of citational doubling without the controlling rudder of an utterance that is not already the consequence of the citational procedure.

Within the poem's abyssally folded frame is written an epistemological meditation that reflects the impulsive desire of Ulysses to sail through the limitations of the known to an absolutely transcendent unknown. Within the limits of knowledge, the unknown is apparently marked only by absence, and it is this absence that impels Ulysses outward on his voyage. In the poem's second canto, this impulsion—a desire to purify the dialect of the tribe (the goal of Eliot's familiar compound ghost)—is toward a closure of the circuit of speech.

> "There is a human loneliness,
> A part of space and solitude,
> In which knowledge cannot be denied,
> In which nothing of knowledge fails,
> The luminous companion, the hand,
> The fortifying arm, the profound
> Response, the completely answering voice." (OP, 100)

The images here are those of companionship, substantial support, and vocal response—figures of a joining in the totalized circuit of speech. These figures are, however, only felt as disturbances within the loneliness, since they are the "aid of greatness to be and the force." Like the dynamics of a kind of negative theology, these figures of a transcendent outside generate Ulysses' search by providing the "inner direction on which we depend." Desire discloses the difference that organizes poetry's voyage, the differential energy that is its faring forward. It is the human wish that provokes the interminable adventure of the instinctive poem.

The "true creator, the waver / Waving purpling wands" is the third canto's trope of this deferred greatness, which will arise when the circuit of speech is closed, when the exile of loneliness is transcended. The image is of the dominant, creative, romantic self, a figure repeated by the "unnamed creator" of the fourth canto and the "Master" of the sixth. We hear in this figure the "blessed rage for order" of "The Idea of Order at Key West,"

> The maker's rage to order words of the sea,
> Words of the fragrant portals, dimly-starred,
> And of ourselves and of our origins,
> In ghostlier demarcations,
> Keener sounds. (CP, 130)

This early poem reflects the same desire for "the completely answering voice" that is the impulsive force behind Ulysses' voyage. This desire would find satisfaction in the appearance of the one true creator, in the joining of the voice with an answering "luminous companion" from beyond its constraining horizon.

The journey outward, then, is another voyage toward the sun, the luminous companion that figures transcendent illumination and knowledge. It is a journey, as the fourth canto implies, beyond the boundaries of the mystical—a demystifying, epistemological voyage whose payoff is a literal truth that, when known, will bring

> "A freedom at last from the mystical,
> The beginning of a final order,
> The order of man's right to be
> As he is, the discipline of his scope
> Observed as an absolute, himself." (OP, 101)

This journey toward the literally true thus appears as a voyage out from the improvised fabrications of poetry and metaphor toward the center of the self. And yet the terminus of the voyage in a pure, demystified beginning is, as the extended mediation that opens the canto suggests, never other than a beginning again within those fabrications.

> "The unnamed creator of an unknown sphere,
> Unknown as yet, unknowable,
> Uncertain certainty, Apollo
> Imagined among the indigenes
> And Eden conceived on Morningside." (OP, 101)

The desired center of knowledge marks not a freedom from the mystical but rather a return of the imagined and conceived, just as, in "Notes," the unmediated perception of the sun in its "remotest cleanliness" reveals only the conception of that sun as the contrived "idea of it," as the product of a methodological procedure (CP, 381, 380). Desiring the center beyond the horizon of the mystical, Ulysses searches for what is originally a mystifying metaphor. The hypothesis that opens his soliloquy conceals this subreption disclosed in the fourth canto, for its belief in the unity of being and knowing is based upon the structure of figurative language itself. Its horizon is the logic of metaphoric substitution (being for knowledge) and metonymic expansion ("to know one man is to know all"). It is only within this textual horizon that knowledge (the "only sun of the only day") emerges, just as, in *The Family Reunion*, the sun appears only in the metaphoric circulation of the South. Knowledge, for both Eliot and Stevens, is the essentially practical, local consequence of a textual or methodological procedure.

The forever-foretold closure of Ulysses' voyage through metaphor appears in Canto V specifically as a closure of symbolic language upon the thing symbolized, the object lying over the horizon of the symbolic—as, in other words, the arrival of the vehicle of metaphor at a literal tenor or central meaning. This is the life that is "always . . . another life,"

> "A life beyond this present knowing,
> A life lighter than this present splendor,
> Brighter, perfected and distant away,
> Not to be reached but to be known,
> Not an attainment of the will
> But something illogically received,
> A divination." (OP, 101)

This life is that of demystified, totalizing truth, the "Omnium" that descends

> . . . "the day on which the last star
> Has been counted, the genealogy
> Of gods and men destroyed.
> The ancient symbols will be nothing then.
> We shall have gone behind the symbols
> To that which they symbolized." (OP, 102)

The canto ends, however, with a startling qualification, for on that day we shall have journeyed "Away / From the rumors of the speech-full domes" to another "chatter that is then the true legend." Here the difference between symbol and symbolized is complicated, for this passage does not take us beyond the horizon of symbol but rather returns us to a symbology that retells legends of the end of its unjustified rumors. This difference organizes two moments of legend, two manifestations of "chatter," but blurs the apparently simple distinction between a rumor and the truth. The divination is the story of the literal truth of symbol, but that truth is another legend of truth, another "speechfull dome," or rhetorical improvisation.

The genealogy of symbols, whose end was foretold in Canto V, returns in the sixth canto as the only possible structure of knowledge.

> "The mind renews the world in a verse,
> A passage of music, a paragraph
> By a right philosopher: renews
> And possesses by sincere insight
> In the John-begat-Jacob of what we know,
> The flights through space, changing habitudes." (OP, 103)

This genealogical pattern, in which are deployed origins, fathers, and generations, becomes the law for which Canto VII provides several manifestations. It is not a law as in natural law or universal principle but a procedure, a repeated methodological organization that produces the things that are known. Each of its subsequent manifestations repeats a structure in which particulars are bent "to the abstract" and are made to organize themselves around that abstraction as though it were their natural center and origin.

> . . . "the difficult inch,
> On which the vast arches of space
> Repose, always, the credible thought
> From which the incredible systems spring,
> The little confine soon unconfined
> In stellar largenesses." (OP, 103)

Each abstraction is a return of the giant, a return of the image of a transcendent presence lying beyond (or beneath, as a controlling center) the incredible systems it fathers. But each is itself a systematic production of the genealogical law whose end Canto V foretold. This, then, is the "fate that dwells in truth": that all truths, all abstractions are produced systematically, methodologically, and repeatedly by the coaxings of a rhetoric that organizes them according to the paradigm of the "genealogy / Of gods and men," in terms of a divine origin and its various derivations. Truths cannot be determined without this pattern of organization, but, for Stevens, it is the paradigm itself that has no ultimate justification. As an earlier poem asked, "Where was it one first heard of the truth?" Its answer, "The the," interrupts the neutrality of the truth by returning it to the "dump" of images (CP, 203).

The final canto of the poem reflects another manifestation of the coaxing law of Canto VII. The old figure of the giant, the metaphor of transcendent presence and sibylline author of all divinations and texts, had been the "englistered woman," but Ulysses is satisfied that he has left that worn-out "old shape" behind.

> "What is the shape of the sibyl? Not,
> For a change, the englistered woman, seated
> In colorings harmonious, dewed and dashed
> By them: gorgeous symbol seated
> On the seat of halidom." (OP, 104)

The new shape that plays the role of sibyl is "the sibyl of the self, / The self as sibyl." This substitution, however, does not result in the arrival of the self "as he is," as foretold by Canto IV. Rather, the return is that of the self as sibyl, the self as newest symbol of a sibylline authority produced and kept in play only by the repeated circulation of symbols and the methodological procedure that organizes them. Here is no discovery, but another production. In the final lines of the canto, the subreption of the worn-out symbol follows the "project for the sun" of "Notes" by becoming the sign of a "still inhuman more," of a transcendence projected by "our features, known / And unknown." This is the final sublimation of the poem, a divination (in the sense of "making divine") of the human in a symbol that is then seen as a sign of transcendence. This procedure, in which are differentiated the human and the divine, the known and the unknown, the symbolic and the literal, is thus a deployment of difference that produces the things that are different as methodological constructs similar to the "big figures" of physics Stevens elsewhere describes as "statistical illusions."[6] Ulysses' epistemological voyage is a lateral drift between these illusions.

That all identities are produced only by the repeated deployment of difference as a methodological procedure is demonstrated no

---

6. Wallace Stevens, "Three Manuscript Endings for 'A Collect of Philosophy,'" in Frank Doggett and Robert Buttel (eds.), *Wallace Stevens: A Celebration* (Princeton, 1980), 56.

more surprisingly than in a poem whose title suggests the absolute identity of a freely constructing imagination not subject to methodological constraints. The poem, called "Human Arrangement," finally reveals the bound status of the arrangement, the edifice, in which being, will, and fate are first "forced up from nothing" (CP, 363). This is no human arrangement, no intentional product of a willing being that, as it turns out, is produced by the arrangement itself, but is rather the repetition of an irrevocable procedural law, of a "Rain without change within or from / Without." The arrangement is thus not a free act of the mind but is rather

> Place-bound and time-bound in evening rain
> And bound by a sound which does not change,
>
> Except that it begins and ends,
> Begins and ends again. (CP, 363)

This constraining and unchanging sound is characterized, in "Large Red Man Reading," as an unneutralizable textuality whose pervasiveness recalls the epistemological constraints of "The Sail of Ulysses" (CP, 423–24). In this poem, it is only within the confines of a text, between the constraining covers of the "purple tabulae" the large red man reads, that are traced the "outlines of being and its expressings, the syllables of its law," the "vatic lines" of "*Poesis, poesis.*" Identity and its different manifestations are the products of a law, the practical consequences of a reading procedure. Like Ulysses, whose mind is a text that discloses the recitative character of his supposedly free and original speech, the large red man reading names a poetic pretext that is at the same time a textual effect.

Stevens' writing demonstrates that an unconstrained and innocently true writing—the dream of the conservative fictionist—can never be written. Since all truths are constituted only through a sorting procedure or a deployment of difference that marks the return of methodological arrangement, a neutral, innocent, and universal truth can be nothing other than a perplexing problem. What we will always be needing, as "Things of August" tells us, is "A new text of the world" in which "The meanings are our own," a writing whose significance "comes from ourselves," free of question or interference, "Because we wanted it so," because we will certain distinct meanings to be present there (CP, 494–95). But such a text, the poem goes on to suggest, is always interfered with by the constraints of its production; it "had to be" and therefore cannot be the simple representation of a willing intentionality, for its appearance is also a sign of its coercively constrained production and of its status as another old text whose meanings may be accidental and not simply our own. The recitation of this old text is the redeployment of the differentiating procedure, or methodological law, that is in the end necessary for us to think, since, the poem concludes, thinking occurs only by "writing and reading the rigid inscription." The purely derivative and distinctly recitative character of all articulations of truth, significance, and meaning can, as Stevens' writings demonstrate, never be neutralized. What we always lack, in other words, is a meta-language uncomplicated by methodological constraints.

When Stevens writes in "An Ordinary Evening in New Haven" of "disillusion as the last illusion," he deploys the difference that organizes all thinking and all writing (CP, 468). The margin that passes between disillusion and illusion is the same one that articulates truth and falsity, the literally real and the fictively metaphoric, but it is a margin that both distinguishes between disillusion and illusion and negates the ultimate justification for the distinction. If disillusion can appear as "the last illusion," then it names not simply the outside or corrective opposite of illusion but also its illusionary inside. Similarly, the distinguishing margin between disillusion and illusion must be simply a methodological construct that suggests the determinate difference between illusion and disillusion while simultaneously negating the absolute identity of either. In the fifth canto of "New Haven," everything begins (and is always already begun) in an illimitable chain of illusion, an Eliotic river or a Peircean infinite chain of signs, never arrested or limited by disillusion. This beginning is not simply the reiteration of illusion. It is also the redeployment of the difference, the repetition of the differentiating procedure, in which illusion and disillusion are differentially constituted.

The dynamics of this difference is traced by the leaves in the twelfth canto of "New Haven," which mark the space "between," out of which emerges the "whole psychology" of individualized presences.

The mobile and the immobile flickering
In the area between is and was are leaves,
Leaves burnished in autumnal burnished trees

And leaves in whirlings in the gutters, whirlings
Around and away, resembling the presence of thought,
Resembling the presences of thoughts, as if,

In the end, in the whole psychology, the self,
The town, the weather, in a casual litter,
Together, said words of the world are the life of the world. (CP, 474)

This canto opens with a discussion of the "res," a figure that has traditionally been taken as the name of an eternal present that words speak about, a transcendent identity—self, world, life—reflected by, but finally distinguishable from, language and poetry. Such determination, however, becomes inoperative if, as Stevens writes, "The poem is the cry of its occasion, / Part of the res itself and not about it." Both referent and reference, transcendent signified and poetic signifier, the res is a site of difference in which presence and representation endlessly shift places. Since the poem is part of this res, its "occasion" is the making of this difference, one local reiteration of the differentiating procedure, and its "cry" suggests the essential difference that constitutes it and not the simple re-presentation of a transcendent identity. The poem is a "cry that contains its converse in itself," a differential "perpetual reference" or interreferential field, in which the things that are different— words and things, references and referents—change places in a continual inversion and iteration without first or last term. This perpetual reference, which recalls Eliot's dissertation, in which an "idea *is* (not *has*) a reference," constitutes the poem's dynamic life (CP, 473, 471, 466; KE, 93).

In this manner whatever figure named by the poem as its origin is brought into play as the product of the poem's differentiating procedure. In "New Haven," this figure is often that of the self: "Suppose these houses are composed of ourselves." Further, in Canto XXII, the "philosopher's search / / For an interior made exterior" and "the poet's search for the same exterior made / Interior" is incited by the sense of "original cold / And original earliness." The search is for a resolving origin, a first referent, uncomplicated by the "perpetual reference" of a belated poetic or philosophic discourse. But the Stevensian search never results in an affirmation of such an origin. Rather, the indispensable sense of origin is for Stevens a component of the search itself, a reiterated figure of an impossible discovery. It is a rhetorical device, a strategic move, that reinscribes the difference essential to the ancient cycle of desire that keeps poetry and philosophy going. What Stevens affirms here is the productiveness of the search, a figure much like Eliot's faring forward, and the essential difference that is its dynamics. It is a search whose products we always see but whose differentiating dynamics can be repeated but not represented (the result is always another methodological "presence").

As Canto IX states, "We keep coming back and coming back / To the real," and thus the poetic search is always for

The poem of pure reality, untouched
By trope or deviation, straight to the word,
Straight to the transfixing object, to the object

At the exactest point at which it is itself. (CP, 471)

But this "real," like the methodological reality of Stevens' adage about the circulation of metaphor, is a perplexing figure of both the literal object and the metaphoric word, a conduplicated "cry that contains its converse in itself" and is so complicated that "we cannot tell apart / The idea and the bearer-being of the idea" (CP, 466). Word/object, bearer-being/idea, metaphoric vehicle/signified tenor —these are the binary oppositions in which the search for an original pre-text outside of the perpetual reference of the poem takes place, but it is a search that denies the justification of its essential terms. Since, as this second canto suggests, the determining line between signifier and signified can never be rigorously drawn, this simple opposition must have only methodological significance, and thus the endlessly repeated search for the literal idea believed to be carried by the metaphoric vehicle of the word deploys this distinction only as a problematic part of its own procedure and not as a transcendent, universal truth.

The first canto's meditation upon the figure of the "version," here an apparently vulgar account of an ideally proper experience from which the eye's vulgate is derived, repeats the binary oppositions (signifier/signified, metaphoric vehicle/literal tenor, derived word/ original object) conventionally employed in all discussions of language. To these oppositions, however, "New Haven" adds the interference of "a few words, an and yet, and yet, and yet" of Stevens' "never-ending meditation" that makes a difference to these oppositions even as it repeats them. These oppositions traditionally describe language (they constitute the meta-language of language), and Stevens' poetry often meditates upon this meta-language. The question posed in these meditations is the one broached in this first canto: "Of what is this house [three lines later described as "words, lines, not meanings, not communications"] composed if not of the sun [?]" (CP, 465). Can we think of language in terms other than those of the container and the contents, the house and the sun, the derived version and the proper object, or the bearer-being and the idea—that is, in terms other than those of the genealogical law of origins and derivatives, the law of re-presentation? If these oppositions cannot be used to describe language, what can? If words and lines are "not meanings, not communications," if they are "dark things without a double" and therefore not composed "of the sun" of meaning, of what are they composed? Stevens here suggests that words cannot be thought of as deriving from an ideal meaning existing as a "thing apart." It is this classical understanding of words that here represents the meaningless. Rather, meanings and communications are produced by words and lines only through an interminably differentiating procedure—only, that is, through the redeployment of the differential relationship in which one methodological giant makes a difference to another, or a "second giant kills the first." Within this never-ending differentiation, multiple meanings are always produced, but no meaning stands as a transcendent, individualized identity unaffected by other meanings. In the clash of the giants of meaning, it is the differential relationship in which they emerge, the killing of the one by the other, that constitutes the dynamics of meaningful language. Thus each new sun, each successive giant of meaning, is itself not the central and controlling sun of Platonic rhetoric, not the real and proper experience from which the improper version can be said to derive, but another eccentric version, "a recent imagining of reality, / / Much like a new resemblance of the sun," or like "another image at the end of the cave." Each redeploys difference; it is only the form that difference takes and the identities it constitutes, the difference between version and reality, that Stevens ultimately negates with his perpetually differentiating "and yet's" that suggest the dynamic and eternal return of difference.

To read Stevens, then, is to trace the differentiations of "this endlessly elaborating poem" in which the "theory of poetry" is displayed as "the life of poetry" (CP, 486). In the twenty-eighth canto of "New Haven," Stevens sets his poem apart from that of the "more harassing master" whose proof would be that

> . . . the theory
> Of poetry is the theory of life,
>
> As it is, in the intricate evasions of as. (CP, 486)

This proof repeats the classical theory of metaphor as the communicating vehicle for a literal tenor that checks its evasions; it emphasizes the things that are different and obscures the difference that constitutes them. Here poetry is seen as a language whose "intricate evasions of as," whose detour into the differentiations of figure and metaphor, finally lead to an end in the revelation of "life, / / As it is." But Stevens' "endlessly elaborating poem" recites this theory with a difference that interrupts its opposition between *as* and *is,* for in this poem the "theory of poetry" does not figure a metaphoric detour leading to the outside of metaphor but rather marks a life saturated by the differences metaphors redeploy.

For Stevens, the meta-language of poetic theory can itself be displayed as a metaphor for the "life of poetry," for it deploys the constituting difference in which theory and practice, critical metalanguage and poetic language, the higher science of commentary and its textual subject, originally emerge interreferentially as the difference each makes to the other. "This endlessly elaborating poem" suggests the complicated dynamics of a poetic labor that, like Ulysses' sail and the metaphoric voyage, deploys the differences it both relies on and desires to close. Where inside and outside, metaphor and literality, poetry and commentary, continually shift places—where the margin that articulates these identities has only a problematically methodological justification—writing and poetry can only appear as an endlessly elaborating and differentiating voyage of figure and trope that cannot finally be described as beginning in or arriving at a secure and uncomplicated haven of the literally true or the centrally significant. In Stevens' writings, as in Eliot's *Four Quartets,* the poetic voyage in the *as* of metaphor describes an interminable adventure.

Anything we say about anything is a metaphor, the substitution of one experience for another. Every definition is always "in other words."

—Fred Alan Wolf

A difference must exist [for work to be accomplished].

—Jeremy Campbell

Afterword
Haphazard Denouement

The poetries of Eliot and Stevens are not each wholly unique and independent. Rather, they overlap, and the site of this overlap is the site of a problem: the eternal return of difference. Their poetries do not speak with two voices about a single identity immanent in both but suggest the essential difference with which all thinking, all writing, originally emerges. Where Eliot and Stevens overlap and repeat each other, there is the site not of identity but of interference and the redeployment of difference. This is the differential energy that characterizes both poetries and is readable in both Eliot's Christianized rhetoric of the incarnation and in Stevens' endlessly elaborating hesitations and qualifications. This energy is readable not as an identity contained in both but as the procedure of differentiation that deploys difference insistently and repeatedly, setting in perpetual motion the poetic, linguistic, and cognitive life of both poets' writings. Like thermodynamic engines, these poetries are kept alive and working by a Pentecostal fire in Eliot and a book-burning, auroral effulgence in Stevens. Both fires break down identities and release the differential energy they obscure.

But poetic work in Eliot and Stevens is not simply destructive or deconstructive, for the redeployment of difference is productive; to make a difference, to put difference to use, is to produce the things, the individualized cognitive identities, that are different. In Eliot we drowse by the fire and envision the underpattern in which differences collapse to unity; in Stevens we speculate in summer, when we are half-asleep, on the hypothesis of reality. But these identities are produced by the poetic work that also discloses their improvisational, illusory, and differential constitution; the host has his complementary parasite, but the parasite also has his complementary host. Messages, meanings, identities, are always being spoken by both Eliot's and Stevens' poetries, but only along with the unfilterable noise of their production, with the randomness and interference that interrupts their ultimate justification. It is within this dynamic, differential relationship that noise and message, improvisation and intention, difference and identity, metaphoric trope and literal meaning, are constituted, not as individualized identities but as uncertain complements that overlap. Either poet could have written the epigraphs to this afterword, though the first comes from a discussion of quantum mechanics and the second from a book on thermodynamics and information theory. Yet the authors of these epigraphs share with the poets the insistence upon difference that pervades twentieth-century physics, philosophy, and literature. For this reason, Stevens and Eliot are distinctly twentieth-century writers; due to their manners of distinguishing difference, we might even call them postmodern or post-Newtonian. Theirs are not poetries of cognitive certainty but are rather adventures in writing and thinking—lateral slidings from one uncertain cognition, one metaphor, one differential siting, to another—that have a payoff, not in some static and rectifying meaning or intention, but only in the repetition of the productive dynamics of the adventure itself.

Thus in Eliot and Stevens we can trace the eternal return of the same, but we must also recognize that "same" is a pure difference or a differentiating procedure. Our readings must therefore exhibit a radical complementarity; they must simultaneously speak of both identity and of the difference that is its disruptive complement. There is no synthesizing solution to such a hermeneutical complementarity; there is only the redeployment of it, and thus our commentaries must, like the poetries they discuss, come to nothing but a practical end. This is the critic's ancient cycle of desire, his faring forward from one methodologically improvised certainty to another and his redisclosure of the uncertainty on which all such cognitive coherencies depend. His is not a univocal re-presentation of difference in Eliot and Stevens but rather an energetic redeployment of difference as the essential problem of writing.

Index

166; "The Man on the Dump," 169; "Human Arrangement," 170; "Large Red Man Reading," 170; "Things of August," 170–71; "An Ordinary Evening in New Haven," 171–75

Tennyson, Alfred, 34
thermodynamics, 124, 177, 178

via negativa, 156, 157, 158
Von Duyn, Mona, 118

Weiss, Theodore, 39
Weyl, Hermann, 11
Whitehead, Alfred North, 39
will to power, 91, 97, 113, 126, 127